Reflections On Years Gone By

Clifton Edward Collins Sr.

Reflections On Years Gone By

Published by Clifton Edward Collins Sr.
Yorktown, Virginia
Copyright © 2023 by Clifton Edward Collins Sr.
ISBN 979-8-988-3890-0-2

Dedication

To my children and grandchildren.
You are the love of my life, forever!

Tribute

To My Parents
Clifton Herman Collins
(December 27, 1918-May 16, 1999)
Maggie Virginia Collins
(May 29, 1918-August 24, 1983)
and
To My Wives
Viola Vernell Burrell (married 1960–2002)
Brenda Edmonds-Brown (married 2002-present)

The best examples of kindness, love, and care for family,
friends, and other human beings.

True Christian love.

Contents

Introduction

For more than twenty years, I have desired to write my life story. The onset of the coronavirus pandemic in 2020 provided me the time and focus to get it done. The main target audiences are my children and grandchildren, or any young person who may glean bits of beneficial information for their life journey.

What I convey in this book is based on Biblical teachings and personal experience. In other words, much of what I say is what has worked for me over my eighty-three years of life. Only because of God's grace and mercy am I able to share this information with the reader. I made some serious mistakes in my lifetime, and I hope to take some of those mistakes to my grave, shared only with God. No two people or situations are the same, so what worked for me may not work for you. But, hopefully, every reader will take something of value from my experiences.

Though my perception of self may be flawed by conceit, over-confidence, or some other personal quirk, I am a people-person who cares about the welfare of every individual as it relates to their professional and personal goals. My greatest asset is the ability to deal with people of all persuasions and statuses. I try to have a positive impact on every person I meet, and that love and concern need not be reciprocal. We need God's presence in our lives to perfect our relationships. Let's tell all our loved ones—wife, children, parents, sisters, brothers, and friends—we love them and show it.

Being raised by Christian parents, I accepted Christ at the age of thirteen. By twenty-one, I had finished college, gotten married, and gone into the military. By thirty, I had a wife and six children to love, care for, and support. By forty-two, I had completed two tours of combat in Vietnam and retired from the military after twenty-one years of service. At sixty-one, I retired from the Federal Civil Service. At sixty-two, my wonderful wife of forty-one years, Viola, left to be with the Lord. At sixty-three, I married another wonderful lady, Brenda, who has two children. Now at the age of eighty-three, I have a wife, eight children, eighteen grandchildren, eight great-grandchildren, four siblings, lots of friends, and a blessed retired life.

Society's way of viewing the male and female roles in a marriage has changed since I raised my children. In my earlier years, the husband was the provider and protector, while the wife's life dealt primarily with the home and children. Today, quoting the late Dr. Myles Munroe, the "women are bringing home not only the bacon but also the pig." But, no matter how society changes, God and His Manual for living, the Holy Word, will never change. I strongly believe that God still holds the man responsible to lead and be the foundation for the family. If the foundation is weak, then the entire family structure is weak. The man is responsible for the well-being of his family.

Chapter 1

God Gets All the Credit

From the very beginning, I give praise and honor to my Lord and Savior, Jesus Christ for ordering my steps throughout my life. He guided me as a young Black boy in a hostile world. I attended secondary school and excelled despite myself. I attended college, followed by my four sisters and brothers, and we all graduated. My siblings and I remain congenial, caring, and loving.

I can testify to the following:

God is truly Omnipresent (all-present). There isn't a location I can travel to where I can escape His presence. Psalm 139:7-12 describes God as being everywhere.

God is truly Omnipotent (all-powerful). There is no greater power in existence than the power of God, and there is nothing in existence that God doesn't have power over. Deuteronomy 4:37 talks about God's "great strength," and in Genesis 17:1, the Lord says to Abram, "I am God Almighty."

God is truly Omnibenevolent (all-good). God has truly showered me with His blessings. God's goodness is found throughout the Bible. John 3:16 states, "For God so loved the world, that He gave His one and only Son, that whoever believes in Him shall not perish but have eternal life." Luke 18:19 says, "So Jesus said to him, 'Why do you call Me good? No one is good except God alone.'"

God is truly Omniscient (all-knowing). God knows everything. There isn't a single thing that can be known, past, present, or future, that God isn't aware of. In the Book of 1 John 3:20, it says that "God is greater than our heart, and He knows everything."

I thank God for blessing me with loving and supportive parents, siblings, and extended family members. He coupled me with wonderful, God-fearing wives and put in my heart to be faithful and love them through whatever we encountered. He graciously allowed me to be a father to eight generous and caring children whom I adore. God also blessed me with reasonably good health at eighty-three years of age and to be cancer-free for nineteen years.

God, the Father, the Son, and the Holy Spirit has been with me all the time, even when I traveled cross-country numerous times in various overloaded vehicles with wife, six kids, a dog, and a cat and with suitcases stacked three-high on top. In the heat of the Mohave Desert or snowcapped mountains of Pennsylvania, God rode along. He was with me through two tours in Vietnam when death and carnage were all around. God also covered my family during my absences from home.

I am Truly Blessed

My journey or route in life was determined by God. There was no way I could have known or mapped out the activities of my life. I had no idea I would be married consecutively to two wonderful wives for a current total of sixty-one years and have eight lovable children.

Moreover, I thank God for providing me the skills and ability to endure and do well in school. I always had the desire to read and figure out things. My love of reading centers around nonfictional books and articles. A subscription to the National Geographic Magazine and books of that genre are my favorites even today. The first serious book I read as a youngster, and therefore the most memorable, was about the life of John Quincy Adams, our sixth president. The impact of that book on my life had nothing to do with President Adams per se, but it was my first major exposure to the world beyond the Eastern Shore of Virginia.

Please be mindful there was no television, nor were we receiving a newspaper during my youth. All we had was radio news. Famous announcers such as Edward R. Murrow, Walter Cronkite, and Paul Harvey come to mind. Later, my parents purchased a set of encyclopedia books, and I truly enjoyed reading those.

My desire to be inquisitive was an important incentive for my progress. I never enjoyed reading about or viewing violence, therefore, a military career was the furthest thing from my mind. I wanted to fix people and things. I even considered becoming a doctor primarily because the only Black man who appeared to be prospering and living the so-called good life on the Eastern Shore near my home was Dr. James Allen. But, after I realized being a doctor meant being around lots of blood, becoming a mathematician became my life's ambition, as noted in my high school yearbook.

Life circumstances dictated that I spend twenty-one years in the military first. A military career had its ups and downs, but overall, it was a blessing. Perhaps the greatest blessing was to have survived and now reap the benefits of military retirement. We have complete medical coverage and retirement income and privileges. During my military service the family and I traveled and enjoyed the world by air, land, and water with only a few minor incidents, but no serious accidents.

Subsequently, I was blessed with an enjoyable Federal Civil Service job for nineteen years involved in the application of mathematics and statistics, and an additional lifetime retirement. To not miss a paycheck in sixty years is a true blessing. I don't think any other career pattern would have made my life journey any more rewarding or enjoyable.

As I reflect on my working life, I notice a trend. Whenever I worked for a "winner," my evaluations reflected a "winner." When I worked for a "loser," my evaluations reflected a "loser."

As an example, the worst evaluation I ever received in the military came from a supervisor who had been passed over for promotion so many times he was still a captain after eighteen years in the Army. Normally, officers are promoted to captain after only four years.

One of the best evaluations I ever received in the military was written by a three-star lieutenant general. The same trend revealed itself in my civilian career. The worst evaluation came from the least regarded supervisor, and the best evaluation was written by a star achiever. So, my advice to young people is to "hook your ambition to a star."

I became and remained an active participant in my career development. For instance, if I knew a certain skill, school, or assignment would enhance my career progression, I didn't hesitate to initiate actions to pursue that skill, school, or assignment.

In the military, I was aware relocations and reassignments often took place every three years. Therefore, at the beginning of my third year at a particular location, I submitted my preferences to Headquarters, Department of the Army (HQDA). If I waited for HQDA to determine my next location/ assignment, I would likely receive the leftover opportunities. There were two major exceptions to this scenario. My tour in Germany was cut short when I was ordered to Vietnam for my first combat tour in 1966. Then, while stationed at Syracuse University, I unexpectedly received orders for my second tour to Vietnam in 1971.

I have been on this journey for eighty-three years. As time passes, I have decided to pay others to perform many tasks that I have lovingly performed in the past. I no longer cut my grass, power-wash the house, rake leaves, repair vehicles, etc. I have donated my lawnmower, many tools, and my beautiful bicycle. The doctor doesn't want me to fall off the bike and hit my head (smile).

Of course, these life changes have an impact on the number of resources needed to live a carefree retired life. God foresaw this situation also and provides me with an adequate retirement income to make these life changes.

Lastly, the icing on the cake is the joy of teaching and tutoring mathematics and statistics to young people and adult military and civilian students for the past forty-two years. I enjoy standing in front of a room full of students and teaching mathematics or statistics more than hitting a golf ball or rolling a bowling ball. I plan to continue imparting my math skills for as long as God permits.

Online classes are not as enjoyable because I miss the interaction.

Chapter 2

Major World Events Affecting My Life

My life probably has been less eventful than many other people's lives, however, I am so thankful to be able to talk about my life. Being born in 1939 has given me the opportunity to live through several major world events.

World War II

I was two years old when Japan bombed Pearl Harbor on December 7, 1941, and only six years old when the war ended in 1945. What I remember most was having to pull the window shades every night so the enemy flying overhead wouldn't see the lights and bomb our home. When I began school in 1944, we were periodically directed to sit under our desks as a safety measure in case of a bombing raid. Thank God, the enemy never bomb our home or school.

My father had been directed to report to Richmond, Virginia, for induction into the military to join the war. He failed the medical examination because he deliberately ate a complete package of laxatives the morning before reporting. He would have failed induction anyway due to flat feet (smile).

I remember a relative coming home from the war with a 30-odd-6 bolt-action rifle that had three-inch bullets. My father fired that rifle once a year during the Christmas season. His target was always an old, abandoned house across the field almost a mile from our home. When that bullet struck, we heard the echo. That simple act was thrilling to me. Many years later, after my mother died and, much to my regret, my daddy sold the rifle to an antique dealer.

Integration of Major League Baseball

There were covert efforts to integrate Black players into professional baseball in the early 1900s. Other races were allowed to play, but Black players were excluded. Therefore, if a Black player could pass as Native American or any race other than Black, he could play.

Black people were elated when the integration of Black players into major league baseball took place in 1947. Several local Black players could have easily made the teams. Of course, what happened is revealed in the Jackie Robinson story.

Most of my aunts and uncles had moved to Philadelphia and New York, looking for job opportunities. My parents made at least one trip a year to visit. In 1955, when I was fifteen years old, my father took my brother Melvin and me to a baseball game between the Brooklyn Dodgers and New York Yankees.

We were in the left-field stands and could see Jackie Robinson playing second base and Roy Campanella behind the plate. While the Dodgers were on offense, we saw Jackie Robinson steal home. He had taken a lead well off of third base when the pitcher threw the ball to the base in an attempt to catch him. As soon as the ball left the pitcher's hand, Jackie took off for home plate and beat the third baseman's throw to the catcher, Yogi Berra. That play went down in history.

The Korean War

My memory of the Korean War primarily involves my beloved uncle Bobby. My father's brother, Robert Moses Satchell, was drafted into the Army and served as a military policeman. At the young age of twenty-one, he was killed in a battle on Pork Chop Hill on July 11, 1953, merely sixteen days before the armistice that ended the war.

A little research revealed that Pork Chop Hill had no real strategic or tactical value, but the Chinese and United Nations units, primarily supported by the United States, took turns taking the hill.

I was thirteen years old and vividly remember Uncle Bobby's body being shipped home with instructions that the casket could not be opened, period. His personal effects consisting of whatever was on him when he was killed, such as his wallet, coins, pictures, and a damaged fountain pen arrived at my grandmother's house. My brother Melvin reminds me that it appeared that a bullet had struck the fountain pen. I remember going through his personal effects and feeling the cruelty and finality of war. As a young boy, my beloved twenty-one-year-old uncle's body was apparently so mangled, we couldn't even open the casket. My disdain for war greatly increased.

Robert Moses Satchell (June 20, 1932-July 11, 1953); Thirty-second Infantry Regiment, I Company, Third Battalion, Seventh Infantry Division—Killed in Action

An eight-by-ten portrait of Uncle Bobby hangs on my wall and means a lot to me. He was good looking, funny, loving, and a great guy to be around. He was also a big-time teaser.

For instance, he would buy a loaf of raisin bread from Miss Jean's store on the corner, sit on the steps of our house, and eat in front of us kids without sharing. He would call us to come get the treat and then pull it back from our grasp. Isn't it a wonder how an eighty-three-year-old man can still remember what is seemingly a minor event? That loaf of raisin bread is still on my mind (smile).

School Segregation

While in college, four Black college students sat down at the Woolworth lunch counter in Greensboro, North Carolina, to order coffee, and the sit-in movement was born in 1960.

Young Black students all over America conducted sit-ins throughout the South to demand service at lunch counters, bringing attention to racial inequality in many aspects of American life—education, employment, housing, and healthcare.

Bull Conner comes to mind. He was a city official in Birmingham, Alabama, who was strongly opposed to the Civil Rights Movement. His use of police dogs and fire hoses against demonstrators was notorious.

The integration of schools was a major activity in the 1960s. I graduated from a segregated high school in 1956. During my initial sixteen years of education, including college, every teacher was Black. On the other hand, my cousin Robert Blackwell, who is a couple of years older than I, was raised in Pennsylvania and went through sixteen years of education and never had a Black teacher.

The same holds for my eighty-five-year-old friend Howard Mason. He attended school in New Jersey and never had a Black teacher. Obviously, what was taking place north of the Mason-Dixon Line was quite different from what was taking place in the South.

Murder of Icons during Tumultuous Times

Entering the military in 1961 was the beginning of my daily life in an integrated environment. I was prohibited from participating in equal rights demonstrations and similar activities which were daily occurrences in the 1960s.

In 1963, a quarter of a million Americans, all racial and ethnic groups together, participated in the "March on Washington for Jobs and Freedom." That was the beginning of a tumultuous period when five predominant players in the equal rights movement were murdered within five years.

First, Medgar Evers, a local civil rights leader, was murdered in his driveway in Jackson, Mississippi on June 12, 1963. President John F. Kennedy was murdered in Dallas, Texas, on November 22, 1963. Malcolm X was gunned down in the Audubon Ballroom in New York on February 21, 1965. Martin Luther King lost his life on April 4, 1968, in Memphis, Tennessee, trying to help the garbage workers. Two months later, on June 6, 1968, Senator Robert F. Kennedy was murdered in Los Angeles, California.

The Vietnam War

When the American involvement in the Vietnam War escalated in 1965, I was a captain in the U.S. Army. Consequently, I was ordered to serve two tours in that conflict, 1966-67 and 1971-72. My participation had a significant impact on my life, which I will discuss later.

Election of Governor Douglas Wilder

Douglas Wilder served as the sixty-sixth governor of Virginia from 1990 to 1994 and was the first elected Black governor in the United States of America. My wife, Viola, and I made a monetary donation to his candidacy and were invited to attend his inauguration in Richmond. It was an event to remember.

The Gulf War

My youngest brother Lafayette retired as a major in the Army after serving in the Gulf Wars. When I left home for college, Lafayette was only four years old. He has always been my little brother. Remembering the combat death of our uncle Bobby and my two tours in Vietnam, I didn't relish the realization of my little brother being in combat.

Just as exposure to Agent Orange devastated Vietnam veterans, Iraq and Afghanistan veterans often suffer from the Gulf War Syndrome and Amyotrophic Lateral Sclerosis (ALS).

My application for disability after serving in Vietnam was pretty straightforward based on prostate cancer and heart disease. My brother experienced a difficult time getting his disability approved. After an extended fight with the Veterans Administration concerning the severity of his medical issues, he was eventually granted a 100 percent disability rating.

I encourage veterans and spouses to apply for disability benefits due to participation in the Vietnam and Gulf Wars. Additional qualifying conditions are being added continuously. The application process is very, very simple. Merely visit any Veteran Administration, Disabled American Veteran, or American Legion Office, and you will find very helpful personnel to assist you.

The 1990s

The 1990s had its share of headlines dealing with racial strife—the police beating of Rodney King, Los Angeles riots, Latasha Harlins' murder, and the O. J. Simpson trial.

One that hit too close to home was an incident in Hampton, Virginia. It was a bowling alley brawl between Allen Iverson and friends (all of them Black) and a White group in 1993. Only the Black participants were charged with a crime. Allen Iverson, the eventual Basketball Hall of Famer, received a five-year prison sentence which was overturned a year later, thanks to Governor Douglas Wilder.

Election of President Obama

The election of President Obama was a most joyous occasion. He carried himself in such a manner that people all over the world wished him well. Leaders of other countries thought very highly of him and this country. He was a rock star!

My daughter Kimberly and her family were able to meet him and shake his hand in person. When she called to tell us, she screamed on the phone as though she had truly been with a rock star.

Security for President Obama was of great concern to me. Thank the Lord, he survived eight years of presidency. I was and continue to be awesomely blessed to have been alive when President Barack Obama and First Lady Michelle Obama were in the White House. In my mind, they were the greatest White House occupants ever.

The Coronavirus Pandemic

As I pen this document, we are experiencing the end of the coronavirus pandemic which was acknowledged by the federal government in March 2020. In January 25, 2021, the United States' death toll in ten months exceeded 415,000 and continued to rise.

That number represented more than seven times the death toll of the Vietnam War which lasted a decade. Hopefully, this pandemic will run its course very, very soon. Several of my high school friends have succumbed to this deadly virus. Two high school classmates who were sisters died in the same week. One of my very close boyhood playmates Clarence Reid was in a coma for more than five months before passing. The first vaccine to combat the coronavirus pandemic was approved and administered to the first person in record time on December 14, 2020.

Except for doctor appointments and grocery runs, my wife and I self-quarantined to the house for several months. My brother Melvin experienced some symptoms and joined his wife Leona to be tested. It took five weeks to receive the results which indicated that Melvin was positive and Leona was negative. By the time results were received, Melvin was feeling better, and Leona was really sick. Had the test results been provided earlier, perhaps Melvin would have self-quarantined, and Leona would have been spared. Praise the Lord, they are both doing okay now.

What we are experiencing today reminds me of the polio epidemic during my youth. Polio caused paralysis and great difficulty breathing. There were 15,000 cases of paralysis a year in the United States. President Roosevelt was perhaps the most famous victim, and he started the March of Dimes campaign to help fund the effort to find a cure.

For several decades, no one could figure out a cure or a vaccine to prevent this dreaded disease. If medical personnel even suspected a kid might have polio, they were taken from their families and put into sanitariums.

Finally, in 1955, when I was a junior in high school, Jonas Salk and his team at the University of Pittsburgh developed a vaccine. It took them six years to develop and announce the cure. I remember being given the vaccine on a sugar cube.

The Death of George Floyd

Then on May 22, 2020, it was very difficult to watch as a White police officer pressed his knee into the neck of a Black man who lay helpless, begging the police officer to let him up. Mr. George Floyd pleaded for his life, repeating, "I can't breathe" and calling on his deceased mother.

Even after Mr. Floyd lost consciousness, the knee was not removed for several minutes. His death brought on worldwide protests and rioting in the streets.

I wonder what would have happened if the roles had been reversed that infamous day? Can you imagine a Black police officer pressing his knee onto the neck of a White man begging for mercy? Plus, can you imagine the other three policemen on the scene allowing that to happen?

The Black Lives Matter Movement is active throughout America with protestors marching in the streets. Current newscasts of armed militia groups also marching in the same streets of America confronting the participants in the Black Lives Matter Movement is quite concerning to me.

There is hope! Just as there were White freedom riders in the 1960s, there are White participants in the current protests. So, there is still hope that equality for all will be realized one day.

Inauguration of President Biden & Vice President Harris

As this book goes to press, Joseph R. Biden Jr, and Kamala Harris have been inaugurated as President and Vice President of these great United States of America. Kamala Harris makes history as the first female, first Black and first South Asian vice president.

The mere fact that a Black female has been chosen by our democratic system to serve in the second strongest position in our country reaffirms my faith in the strength of our democracy. Perhaps the words of Martin Luther King Jr. are ringing true. "I look to a day when people will not be judged by the color of their skin, but by the content of their character."

Chapter 3

Family Roots

Maternal Grandparents

Fortunately, my maternal grandparents were alive for nearly the first three decades of my life, and their home was only two miles from us on the same country road. I either got off the school bus at their house or made the trip to visit several times during the week. I spent a lot of time with my grandparents. It's been said that the best gift you can give your children is to allow them to spend time with their grandparents. I believe that to be true.

My parents and grandparents, maternal and paternal, never had to endure the stigma, degradation, and entrapment of living in the White man's house, shopping on credit at his store, and being required to work on his farm. They acquired the knowledge and skills to gain nonfarm employment. Families who found themselves working on the White man's farm didn't earn enough to buy their own home, and they were always in debt at the farmer's store and/or for personal loans. Their children had a small chance of escaping the same cycle, and the family was basically in servitude.

My grandfather Robert David Satchell was very skilled in the home building trades. He trained all male members of our family the skills of carpentry, bricklaying, and painting. Stories were told of his fearlessness of high heights. He was the only carpenter in the family who would scale and repair the towering steeple at the church we attended.

At that time, my grandfather and uncles Earl and James worked for the biggest building contractor on the Eastern Shore of Virginia, who happened to be Black. They built beautiful homes up and down the Delmarva Peninsula.

20

The term Delmarva is short for parts of the States running from north to south of Delaware, Maryland, and Virginia. It's bordered by the Chesapeake Bay on the west and the Atlantic Ocean on the east. Traveling south from Delaware on Highway 13, the peninsula is about 170 miles long and ends at the Chesapeake Bay Bridge-Tunnel. The Bridge-Tunnel is an eye-opening eighteen miles long and ends near the Virginia Beach area.

Uncle Earl even relocated with that contractor when he secured a maintenance contract in Richmond, Virginia. Little did he know that in later years, he would not reap the benefits of loyalty to his employer.

Family gossip was that, although the building contractor withheld social security payments from the men paychecks, he failed to submit payments to the government. Consequently, when my uncle Earl and other relatives went to claim their social security retirement, their entitlements were very minimal.

Since the men in the family had excellent skills, our standard of living was relatively higher than many families in the area, Black or White. We always had adequate food, at least one family vehicle, and an outfit for church on Sunday.

Grandpa "Papa" Satchell was the type of grandfather who didn't interact with kids very well. I was afraid of him until I became a teenager. He wasn't mean, but it seemed he didn't have much to do with small kids. He deemed that to be Grandma's responsibility.

When it came to us kids, he relayed the message or feeling through Grandma. "Noni, stop those kids from slamming that door."

When he got angry, he blinked his eyes rapidly. We nicknamed him "Blinkum" (but never to his face) and stayed away from him as much as possible.

Sitting at the table for dinner was quite interesting. First, our hands had to be in our lap, not on the table. Once Papa said the grace, Grandma served Papa's plate. At that time, we were allowed to raise our hands to accept the serving dishes as the food was passed around the table. Seconds were offered to the kids once Papa had been satisfied. Of course, we weren't allowed to leave the table without permission. I have never regretted experiencing that ritual at the dinner table. That type of structure benefited me throughout my life, including raising my children.

When I was a teenager, I had a few more interactions with my grandfather. Once I took the time to sit down and converse with him, he was an interesting gentleman. Family members often laugh about the stories he

Viewing left to right - Kneeling in front — Granddad Robert Satchell and Aunt Mildred's husband, Uncle Holland Fisher (bride's father); 1st row — Mrs. Lauretta Fisher (Uncle Holland's stepmother), Cousin Lorraine Fisher (bridesmaid), Aunt Mildred Satchell Fisher (bride's mother), Cousin Flossie Fisher (bride), James Jones (groom), Richard H. Jones (father of groom), back row - Mary C. Jones (mother of groom), the presiding minister, my grandmother Elenora Satchell, and Calvin C. Jones (brother of groom).

told. For instance, he spoke of the large watermelons he grew. In describing the size, his hands began twelve inches apart, but by the time the story ended, his hands were three to four feet apart.

My grandfather told a lot of tall tales. I will never forget his story of walking across the Chesapeake Bay on dry land from Cape Charles to Little Creek. According to him, the Chesapeake Bay had dried to the point of allowing a person to walk across vice riding on the ferries. Of course, I have never found any historical records to validate this tale.

Papa's death certificate indicates he was seventy-eight when he died from apoplexy and hypertension. I was always told that he had died of prostate cancer. I know very little about his parents, except they were James Henry Satchell (1849 – 1939) and Mary Ashby (1846 – 1907).

Grandma Elenora Fitchett Satchell
(April 11, 1883 - February 23, 1978)

Grandma Elenora Satchell was the sweetest and gentlest grandmother in the world. She was a beautiful lady with long wavy hair reaching her waist. Although I don't know for a certainty, it appeared to me she had Indian ancestors based on the length and texture of hair and her high cheekbones. My sister Barbara states Grandma told her that her mother was raped by a White man. She doesn't know if that meant her father was White.

Grandma's name in various historical documents is spelled differently—Elenora, Elnora, Ellenora, and Elenore. Her parents of record were George Fitchett (February 1835 – March 16, 1916) and Rachell West (1842 – May 3, 1925).

She was a homemaker who I don't think ever worked outside the home. The closest she came to outside work was washing and ironing clothes for a prominent White family.

That was quite an enterprise to watch. We children pumped the needed water, and she scrubbed the clothes on a washboard. Then, she ran the washed clothes through a vintage Maytag Wringer Washer. Rinse water had a little "bluing" in it, then clothes went through the wringer again, followed by hanging on the clothesline. Later, each outer garment was ironed using metal irons heated on the wood-burning kitchen stove. Oh, how easy we have it today with automatic washers, dryers, and electric irons.

Her daughter, my aunt Edna Wescott, sent her two young sons, John and Leroy, from Philadelphia to live with our grandparents, and they attended elementary and high school on the Eastern Shore.

Of course, caring for two kids all the time and two more part-time (my brother Melvin and me) was a full-time job. John was older, but he played baseball and dodgeball with Leroy, Melvin, and me.

Uncle Earl, his wife Minerva, and three children—Ellen, Gloria, and Earl Jr.—lived next door to our grandparents. Ellen and Gloria were girls and older than I was, and Earl Jr. was too young, so they weren't considered my playmates. John, Leroy, Melvin, and I were the fearsome four who played together.

I don't remember Grandma Elenora whipping us, or perhaps I should only speak for myself (smile). With John and Leroy around, Melvin and I always had playmates. There was a seven-year age spread among us four boys with John being the oldest (DOB 1934), followed by Leroy (DOB 1936), then me (DOB 1939), and Melvin (DOB 1941) as the youngest. We were close enough in ages to play together, with the oldest and the youngest paired up while Leroy and I made our team. We played baseball, dodgeball, marbles, hide 'n' seek, blind man's bluff, and hopscotch, rode bikes, and shot BB-guns until nightfall. Since our bathroom needs were met by use of the outhouse or being in the midst of the forest, there was no reason to return to the house. Technology had not invaded our lives as it has done to youngsters today.

In the 1940s and 50s, my parents didn't own a TV, however, my mother's parents did. It was a ten-inch black and white television, and the big event was for us to visit my grandparents on Sunday afternoon and watch the Boston Blackie Show, I Love Lucy, and the Ed Sullivan Show.

My grandmother always served the best homemade ice cream. The main ingredients were vanilla flavoring, Carnation can milk and a little sugar. Also, she always had pound cake. Whenever there was a special occasion, we could expect to enjoy the hand-cranked ice cream. If you have not had the pleasure of enjoying that treat, please search "hand-cranked ice cream" on the internet to learn more.

I don't remember her being seriously ill at any time. When she had a cold, etc., she always had a home remedy to use. Her legs were very bowed. They must have hurt but I never heard a complaint. Whenever we were hurt or had a cold, she served us portions of tea she concocted from various leaves or roots or placed a hot compress on our chest. If we were stung by a bee or wasp, she instructed us to pee in a cup and pour the urine over the affected area. It worked.

Every night before retiring, she had her toddy of Rock 'n' Rye whiskey. She drove her car until she was ninety-three years old. Her daughter (my mother) convinced her to quit driving for fear that her slow encroachment onto Highway 13 was too dangerous.

Living alone at the age of ninety-four, Grandma called my mother at two in the morning on February 23, 1978, and stated that my mom should come for she was feeling bad. By the time my mom had driven the two miles, Grandma was slumped over on the couch. She suffered a myocardial infarction and passed within fifteen minutes.

Paternal Grandparents

Great-great-grandmother Peggie Satchell (Birth Year about 1842)

My paternal grandparents begin with Great-great-grandma Peggie Satchell. She was twenty-eight years old during the 1870 census and had two daughters, Annie (ten years old) and Hellen (six months old), and one son, Gilmer (eight years old).

I have this two-and-a-half by four-inch picture and on the back, it says, "Helen Smith, Eastville, Virginia, 1½ miles North of Eastville Station." I'm somewhat confused because I'm wondering why her daughter's name is on the back of her picture. Considering that location information two generations later, you would be located exactly where her granddaughter, my grandmother Maggie Satchell, lived.

I've attempted unsuccessfully to solve the mystery in Ancestry.com and elsewhere. During my youth, I gleaned that the slave master or another White person in his household impregnated my great-great-grandmother Peggie with my great-grandmother Hellen Jane Satchell Smith, who was born in 1869 and designated Mulatto.

Grandma Peggie worked for Laban J. Belote, a White farmer, as a servant. I often wondered how my grandmother was a Satchell, then Collins, followed by Satchell again. Now I know. Her grandmother and mother were Satchells. Then she married my grandfather Kenneth Collins followed by marriage to my step grandfather Charles Satchell.

The 1910 census indicates that Great-grandmother Hellen Jane Satchell, a Mulatto, at 27 years old, married my great-grandfather William Smith, a 52-year-old Mulatto, in 1899. Hellen could read and write, but William could not. I note that my great-great-grandmother's name is spelled "Hellen" in Ancestry.com and also on her death certificate, rather than Helen. I have learned that the handwritten census and other historical documents have a plethora of misspelled names and other mistakes, but "Hellen" appears to be correct.

Great-grandmother Hellen Jane Satchell Smith (December 12, 1869-January 20, 1935)

Prior to the advent of cars, it was difficult to attend a school that was far from your home, so school children often resided with relatives near their school. When Hellen was eleven and her sister Mary was nine years old, they boarded with the family of Washington Press to attend school. This makes sense because my father always told me we were relatives of the Press family.

My paternal grandfather, Kenneth James Collins, married my grandmother in 1908. There isn't much to say about my grandfather, perhaps because my father, Clifton Herman Collins, was less than two years old when his father died in 1920.

I located a copy of Granddad Kenneth Collins's military draft exemption approval dated June 5, 1917. He wasn't drafted during World War I. The reason given was his responsibility to care for his wife and one child (that would be my aunt Helen, born August 1915).

Paternal Grandfather Kenneth James Collins (April 25, 1893-February 7, 1920)

My grandmother never mentioned him except to say that he had died from the Spanish Flu, known as consumption during that time. More than 675,000 people died during the great influenza epidemic in 1918-20.

Paternal Grandmother
Maggie Smith Collins Satchell
(November 11, 1891–April 16, 1972)

My grandmother Maggie Smith Collins Satchell was the daughter of Hellen and William Smith and wife to Kenneth Collins. After Kenneth died, she married Charles Satchell.

She was referred to as "Miss Peggie" by family and friends. It may be because her grandmother was named Peggie and it distinguished the two.

As kids, we called Grandma Peggie "Sompay." I think we were trying to say "Grand Peg." On my Aunt Helen's birth certificate, my grandmother is designated as Mulatto. She often spoke of being a cousin to a member of the White "James" family.

I remember my father talking about riding in the horse and wagon with his grandfather William Smith, the husband of my great-grandmother Hellen Jane Smith. My research does indeed identify my great-great-grandfather as William Smith.

Grandma Peggie worked as a maid on the Pocahontas Ferry transporting persons and vehicles across the Chesapeake Bay from Cape Charles to Little Creek, Virginia. She worked two days on, then two days off throughout my secondary school years. I will discuss the impact she had on my educational development later.

When I was growing up, nearly every home had at least one apple, pear, or peach tree, plus a grapevine. We could always find fruit to eat every day of the spring and summer. There was always some type of vegetable available, which I will discuss later.

My siblings and friends loved to wander around Grandma Peggie's home because of the abundance of wonderful fruit. Behind the house was a small farm area lined with fruit trees. Included were green apples, red apples, small pears, large pears, and peaches, and in the front yard was a bush that yielded large figs. Near the orchard area were watermelons, cantaloupes, and cucumbers. Wild bushes of honeysuckles and blackberries edged the driveway past her house. Couple the availability of wonderful healthy fruits with virtually every wonderful vegetable you can think of, and we were truly blessed. I'm thankful for the long healthy lives my siblings and I have had. We range from seventy to eighty-three years of age, still in the land of the living.

Grandma Peggie also had some beautiful hydrangea bushes of several colors in the front yard. They were absolutely gorgeous.

After Granddad Kenneth Collins died in 1920, Grandma Peggie remained single until she married my step-grandfather Charles Moses Satchell on December 29, 1927. Granddad Satchell was a retired Pullman porter who worked on railroad sleeper cars. He was a widower and a kind gentleman who had stories to tell about his travels.

When he married my grandmother, he had two daughters, Betty Satchell and Elizabeth Lola Courtney. Elizabeth, who we referred to as Lola, had two children: Siliane and Carson, who we referred to as Snoots.

Granddad Charles's friends called him Cousin Charlie, but we referred to

Step-grandfather Charles Moses Satchell (August 21, 1884–August 3, 1955)

him as "Suhsaw." Please don't ask where that name came from.

Suhsaw fathered one child with my grandmother—Robert Moses Satchell, who I discussed earlier as being killed in the Korean War.

While my grandmother worked on the ferries, he kept the household. He was a wonderful cook, and I always marveled at how he could clean a pork chop bone cleaner with a fork and knife than I could with my teeth. His Pullman training made him a nice, well-mannered and pleasant person to be around.

Since my grandmother worked on the ferries, she was insured medically by the Merchant Marine industry. I remember traveling with Dad to various medical appointments in the Norfolk area for several years. When she died in 1972, my tour in Vietnam was cut short in order for me to attend her funeral.

Parents

My parents were Clifton Herman Collins and Maggie Virginia Satchell Collins. They resided on the Eastern Shore of Virginia until their death.

Clifton and Maggie Collins, Eastville, Virginia, circa 1970

Father

Clifton Herman Collins
(December 27, 1918–May 16, 1999)

My father was chubby in his youth and acquired his lifelong nickname of "Fattie." He was friendly, kind, loving and funny. My father loved our family and was a wonderful provider. He was a friend to everyone he met.

I'm the oldest of five living children. Our brother William died two months after birth. My brothers and sisters in order of age are Melvin, Delores, Barbara, and Lafayette. They have all agreed that we never saw our father angry or heard him talk badly about anyone. He had the best personality of anyone I know and an amazing temperament. I don't remember him ever hollering or screaming at me or my siblings. He simply told us what we had done wrong and whipped us if it was due. I highly respected my father. He made sure our family was cared for and, in my opinion, was an amazing father. Dad was a wonderful father who deeply cared for our family. That's repetitive, isn't it? (smile)

He l..o..v..e..d for Ma to scratch his back with her fingernails. He owned a long wooden backscratcher, and at times, it appeared he was going to injure himself using it.

Dad's formal education ended in the third grade while Ma acquired her high school diploma. I never personally asked my dad, but listening to conversations between my mom and others, it was obvious that my dad's formal education was limited. I never saw him read a newspaper, book, or even the Bible. I always suspected he had difficulty reading, but he could definitely count his money (smile).

Dad didn't concern himself with worldly events. His daily life was centered around a twenty-mile radius of our home, except when he had to travel farther for his job or to visit a relative up north, mostly Philadelphia or New York.

Although the Eastern Shore was primarily farmland, my father never worked on a farm for anyone but himself. He tended a small plot near the house, and of course, Melvin and I were tasked to do most of the physical labor. I remember following a horse either plowing, dragging or cultivating the land. Composted horse and cow manure loaded on a horse-n-cart was spread as fertilizer. Dad grew produce to sell, such as cantaloupes and watermelons, which we loaded onto the flatbed of his truck. As we drove slowly through neighborhoods, we yelled, "Watermelons, cantaloupes!" That was a "fun time" for us youngsters. After I left for college, Dad managed to buy a tractor.

I can't remember a time when my father didn't work. When I was a young boy, my father worked on a crew laying rails for the railroad. My right-handed father and his left-handed partner alternated the swing of their sledgehammers to drive spikes into one-foot square railroad ties. The sound of the sledgehammers on the large spikes was like music to the ears of young boys who marveled at the hammerers' glistening arm muscles.

I don't recall the number of years my dad worked on the railroad, but in time,

My father fabricating concrete pilings used on the Chesapeake Bay Bridge-Tunnel.

the passing trains stopped carrying passengers, then mail, and soon the diminished use of the railway resulted in layoffs.

Dad's next job was with a building supply company (Reliable Lumber Company) in Cape Charles, Virginia. He delivered building materials throughout the Peninsula. He also drove a dump truck to haul coal and often brought the truck home. My brother and I once rode in the back of that dump truck for a visit to a doctor's office in Machipongo, Virginia—a trip of about three miles. I wonder what that doctor thought when we walked in covered with coal dust (smile).

My dad's last job was with the Bay Shore Concrete Products Corporation in Cape Charles, beginning in 1960. That company fabricated the pilings and other cement requirements during the construction of one of the seven engineering wonders of the modern world, the twenty-three-mile-long Chesapeake Bay Bridge-Tunnel.

He spent one day at the construction site on the water. Afterward, Dad informed his supervisor that he couldn't swim, was afraid of water, and would not return. From that day on, he worked at the ground site. The bridge-tunnel was completed in 1964.

Dad was particularly skilled with his hands as a carpenter, bricklayer, and painter. He could fabricate almost anything. For example, he made and sold decorative flower pots out of discarded auto tires and constructed concrete picnic tables which he sold up and down the Atlantic coastline from New York to North Carolina. He was even commissioned by the world-renowned poet Dr. Maya Angelou to provide picnic tables for her backyard in Winston-Salem, North Carolina.

Dad's Popular Picnic Tables in Backyard of Family Homestead

Dad ordered the plastic forms for the picnic table out of a catalog, probably Sears Roebuck. Those forms were used to make perhaps two tables, so Dad came up with the idea of placing the plastic form into a bed of concrete and allowing the concrete to get hard. Once that concrete foundation cured, the plastic forms withstood the completion of numerous tables, thus saving him a lot of money.

While I was stationed in the military at Fort Monroe in the 1970s, Dad often traveled to my home in Hampton, Virginia, with a truckload of those picnic tables. His biggest customers were the hotel owners who put the tables around their outdoor pools. His tables can also be found in Chincoteague and other beach areas up and down the east coast. The only maintenance required is to spray them with a hose from time to time. There wasn't much chance of having them stolen due to their weight.

Dad also supplemented his income by doing odd jobs such as painting houses and repairing fences. One of his main customers was Dr. James Allen, MD, the only Black medical doctor known to me in Northampton County. Dad maintained the doctor's house, his office building next door, the fences, the flower beds, etc.

We, as a family, visited my parents every chance we got over the years. My sister Delores said they loved to see us come because they knew we'd bring a lot of good food. There was a Coast Guard Station near the Chesapeake Bay Bridge-Tunnel entrance at Kiptopeke, Virginia, where we always stopped to shop at the commissary on the way.

The joke as we entered my parents' house was always, "Is there an end to the number of kids coming through the door?"

Dad loved 'himself' some children. He got totally involved in kids' activities. This picture tells the story! Dad with my sister Barbara (right rear) and the grandchildren, circa 1975

My kids loved to visit my parents, especially Dad. While Ma fed and cared for them, Dad did fun things with them. For instance, he sat them between his legs and allowed them to steer the farm tractor or the farm truck.

With certainty, he took them to the Chesapeake Bay or the Atlantic Ocean sites to go crabbing. Their home was less than a mile from an inlet to the ocean and about seven miles from the Chesapeake Bay. The Bay was the ideal place to crab because the beach was sandy, allowing us to walk to the best crabbing spot. The inlet to the ocean area was muddy, so if you couldn't find a pier, you needed a boat.

Dad was so physically strong he could stick both arms out in the form of a cross and allow the kids to swing on them. When Dad flexed his biceps, it displayed an egg-shaped knot. He told the kids he removed that "frog" (knot) each night before going to bed and put it into a dresser drawer. In the morning, he removed the knot from the drawer and replaced it on his arm. They believed him (smile).

There was a little ritual my dad went through every time there was an out-of-town visitor, especially if the visitor was a lady driver. Before they left, he checked their vehicle's readiness for travel—water, oil, and gasoline levels, tire inflation, and lights. If there were any discrepancies, he made the corrections or followed them to the gas station or repair shop to ensure it got done.

Dad was afraid to be out on the water. The story has it that when my dad and his brother Kenneth were young, they skipped school and ventured onto an oysterman's boat salvaging discarded oysters and clams. Without noticing until it was too late, they drifted out from the shore with no oars. Fortunately, they drifted to land several miles down the shoreline.

My father forbade my siblings and me from going anywhere near the ocean or bay, and to my knowledge, none of us ever learned to swim. We didn't need much persuasion after our friend Albert Wright drowned while swimming in the Chesapeake Bay. He was at our favorite spot where we sneaked on occasion, Sand Hill, near the end of Savage Neck Road, Virginia. Albert was the only son of my first-grade teacher.

I have no doubt that my father loved my mother. He hugged her and said sweet things to her because he probably knew he could never replace her in his life. Moreover, my mom was a proud confident lady who demanded respect from my dad and others (smile). My father never raised his hand to my mother and taught me to treat ladies with respect.

After Ma's death in 1983, Dad insisted on staying on the Eastern Shore.

Due to distance, there was no way for us children to know exactly how our dad was doing. Without Ma, my father was completely lost. He was alone with no one to be accountable to.

I often wonder what would have happened to Dad had we, his children, been able to convince him to live with us immediately after Ma's death.

The worst part was the fact that Dad really never had to do housework while Ma was living. He barely knew how to boil water. Cooking was out of the question. There was not a close relative nearby who could fill the void left by my mother. To my knowledge, he did have several friends who helped him do certain tasks.

For instance, a family friend administered his bills, for Dad didn't know how to write checks. I learned later that my sister Delores had completed several checks of various denominations from ten to one hundred dollars that he could use when necessary. I don't think he could read very well. For a while, Dad had a special lady friend who traveled with him when visiting us in Hampton, Virginia. They enjoyed socializing with my family and accompanied Viola and me to several social events.

I was a member of the Les Hommes Social and Civic Club at the time, and whenever there was a bus trip to a football game, I had the bus stop on the Eastern Shore to pick up Dad. He absolutely loved it. I remember very vividly a trip we took to see a New York Giants/Philadelphia Eagles football game. My son Michael and my friend Howard Mason were with us. We managed to visit with Dad's sister Helen in Philly.

At one point, we received word from friends on the Eastern Shore that Dad couldn't locate his car. Later, we learned that Dad drove to the Chesapeake Bay Bridge-Tunnel entrance and was entering the oncoming lane. The gate attendants impounded his car at the tunnel entrance, and a friend in the area who recognized Dad took him home. It took us a while to determine where his car was and what had taken place.

Later, Dad was hospitalized, and when I visited, he asked me to get his black Chevrolet from behind the barn. Well, he had owned a black Chevrolet forty years earlier. We were convinced he needed intervention. He was diagnosed with Alzheimer's at the Baptist Hospital, Winston-Salem, North Carolina, between August 16 and September 27, 1990. He immediately began a rotation of living in turn with Barbara, Lafayette, Delores, and finally in June 1991, he moved into my home.

While Dad was living with me and my family in Hampton, Virginia, he was very easy to please. He never complained about anything, except perhaps how we disciplined our son Michael. As far as he was concerned, his twenty-year-old grandson could do no wrong.

Dad was also crazy about our dog Kimba, a Samoyed dog with beautiful white hair. He always did love dogs; he owned rabbit and coon dogs during my youth.

Dad suffered very badly with arthritis, particularly in his legs. Once he said that he had rubbed his legs with gasoline, trying to get some relief. I was into multi-level marketing at the time and was pushing aloe vera juice and fish oil tablets. After giving Dad aloe vera juice and fish oil tablets, my dad never complained again about pain in his legs.

Dad stayed busy doing something to occupy his time and hands. He raked my yard so much and often that I asked him to please let the grass grow (smile). He also used clothes hangers and twine to make dusters that he sold to family and friends. My sister Barbara taught him how to make beautiful earrings. Of course, he used those to woo the ladies at the senior citizen center. Dad also loved beautiful button covers. He dressed up in a nice pair of pants and shirt, and then covered his shirt buttons with pretty button covers.

When we went out for dinner, he often finished his dinner and found someone at the nearby tables to converse with. Dad would talk to a fence post if it talked back to him. He even dated a pleasant lady for a while. I often took him to her home and returned to pick him up later that evening.

As his duel with Alzheimer's progressed, Dad began to get the time of day confused. For instance, he began to get out of bed, wash up and get fully dressed at three in the morning and wonder why we weren't ready to go somewhere.

It was difficult to witness the deterioration of my father's mental capacity. He had always been physically strong, mentally sharp, and truly the epitome of a good father. His warm personality never changed. He had forgotten my name but the love was still there. Eventually, I deemed it prudent to place him in a nursing home and visited him daily. Whenever I walked into the nursing home, he always said loudly, "Well I be di. Look who's here."

As time passed, he didn't allow his caretakers to shower him, therefore, I had to physically escort him to the shower room. By talking to him while stroking his back, I could get the shower done.

Dad passed while in the Newport News, Virginia, Mary Immaculate Nursing home on May 16, 1999.

Father's Family

My dad was one of seven. His siblings were Helen Collins Rawls, Kenneth James Collins Sr., Raymond Collins, half-brother Robert Satchell and two stepsisters, Elizabeth Lola Courtney and Bettie Satchell Mapp.

Helen Collins Rawls
(Aug 21, 1915–Jun 6, 2007), circa 1950

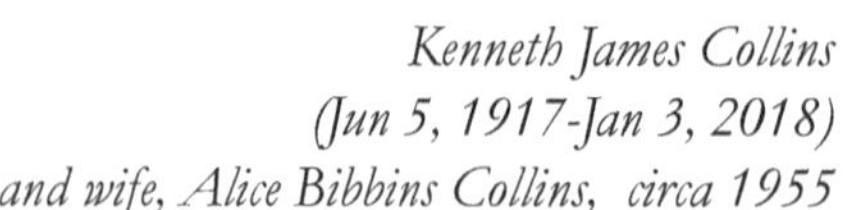

Kenneth James Collins
(Jun 5, 1917-Jan 3, 2018)
and wife, Alice Bibbins Collins, circa 1955

Raymond Collins (Aug 9, 1920–Feb 9, 1980),
circa 1947

*Robert Moses Satchell
(June 20, 1932–July 11, 1953),
circa 1951*

*Viewing left to right: Cousin Siliane
Courtney (June 22, 1926 –April 8,
2013), Aunt Bettie Satchell Mapp
(March 31, 1910-July 16, 2009)
holding my sister Delores, "Skeeter"
(don't remember his real name), and
I cannot identify the lady on the right,
circa 1947.*

Mother

This lady meant the world to me. She was my enforcer, cheerleader, fan, and virtually everything. She was always there for me, made me feel important, had fun with me, taught me to love others, and lastly, administered the disciplinary rod when appropriate. I was truly blessed to have such a sweet, loving, and caring mother.

I will be remiss if I didn't emphasize the importance my mother put on accepting Jesus as our Lord and Savior. My faith in God can be traced back to her. She insisted I attended Sunday school every Sunday. I was not required to stay for the church service; however, if I wanted to go

Maggie Virginia Collins
(May 29, 1918–August 24, 1983)

home after Sunday school, I had to walk nearly three miles home. Being young, I wasn't about to walk home and have to pass through those scary forest areas. In those days, we used the term "woods" to refer to forest areas. I'm sure Ma was aware of my fear. Needless to say, I stayed for church service! During the service, she only had to look my way to keep me on my best behavior. I don't feel that the periodic switch or belt to my behind hurt my development.

Dad had full confidence Ma would do what was best for the family. In addition to working outside the home, Ma ensured we were properly clothed, fed, healthy, educated, disciplined, and respectful of others. She was also a wonderful wife to my father. My father didn't attempt to cook or do any housework. He was always outside making or fixing something. When he came into the house, Ma poured water from the kettle on the stove into a washbasin, and Dad washed his hands and face. Then, he sat at the head of the kitchen table, said the grace, and was served by Ma. Then, Ma allowed the kids to dish out our plates.

Proverbs 31:10-12 says, "A wife of noble character who can find? She is worth far more than rubies. Her husband has full confidence in her and lacks nothing of value. She brings him good, not harm, all the days of her life."

While eating, Dad and Ma exchanged their day's events, and then, Ma informed Dad of the good and not-so-good things we children had done doing the day. If Ma had already whipped us for some infraction, chances were very good that Ma requested that Dad give us a reinforcement whipping. I didn't look forward to those.

Melvin and I would get into bed and hear Dad coming up the stairs. "Your mama told me to give you boys a whipping."

As he attempted to remove our bed covers, we literally hung on for dear life. He merely lifted the quilt or blanket, shook us loose, and commenced the whipping. We often said he shed tears as he administered the discipline. Delores claimed she told Dad that he didn't have to whip her just because Mommy said so. That's hard to believe (smile).

Proverbs 31:13 and 17 says, "She selects wool and flax and works with eager hands. She sets about her work vigorously; her arms are strong for her tasks."

Ma finished high school and did all of the bookkeeping, bill paying, and bank transactions for the family.

Being that I was the oldest child, she taught me how to cook, sew, wash clothes, scrub floors, and other household chores because I was her backup. With her working in the fields and factories, those tasks had to be done. Those of you familiar with Proverbs 31 know that there is probably no woman who can meet all of the characteristics outlined in that scripture, but Ma came close. Her favorite sayings were, "It's a time in the land!" and "Well Do."

Ma worked in the fields, factories, restaurants, or wherever she could get a job. She worked some awful hours, late into the night, weekends, etc. On the Eastern Shore, there were produce graders where workers sorted various vegetables and fruits such as green tomatoes, red tomatoes, pink tomatoes, etc. Each type was loaded onto tractor-trailer trucks destined for markets primarily up north.

In Northampton County, where we lived, there were two factories, the major sources of substantial income for my mother and others. There was James Canning Factory in Kendall Grove, Virginia, near our home, and five miles down the road was the larger G. L. Webster Canning Factory in

Cheriton, Virginia. Those two factories had the best paying jobs, and the workers were not in the fields exposed to the hot sun.

At that time, every kind of vegetable and fruit was grown on the Eastern Shore—white potatoes, sweet potatoes, snap beans, string beans, butter beans, tomatoes, sweet corn, spinach, peppers, strawberries, and others. The vegetables and fruits were harvested at different times in the spring, summer, and fall. Many of those vegetables and fruits were canned or packaged at the two factories and sold all over America.

Ma worked primarily at the G. L. Webster Factory for many years until she and others attempted to unionize the workers. That got Ma and other leaders blackballed, never to work at that factory again. They were relegated to various menial jobs. Even so, I never heard Ma say she regretted her decision because she felt that right was right!

At one point, she worked as a cook at the Eastville Inn and for a business along Highway 13 that sold chicken sandwiches and ice cream.

Proverbs 31:20 says, "She opens her arms to the poor and extends her hands to the needy."

Ma was always helping people, especially the elderly and those in need. Not only did she provide food, but also transportation and other needs. One of her best friends was Isodore "Dubbie" Palmer, a mentally challenged gentleman who loved to be around my mother. He knew that he would get a good meal and be loved and appreciated. Ma always found a chore that Dubbie could do and then invited him into the house to participate as part of our family. Dubbie was always kind to us kids, with never a harsh word.

Proverbs 31:26 says, "She speaks with wisdom, and faithful instruction is on her tongue."

Ma's instructions to me were always wise, encouraging, and for my betterment. She assigned me responsibility in the home which proved invaluable when I had my own family. She taught me how to cook basic meals—eggs and bacon, fried chicken, and vegetables. But there were certain dishes I couldn't duplicate.

The fish man came by every Friday and often Ma bought a large drum fish. I never learned how to prepare the delicious meal that followed. Ma baked the drum fish smothered in gravy, onions, white potatoes, and carrots in a large pan. It was smacking good! Plus, I never learned how to prepare the flapjacks she served on Sunday mornings.

Later in life, I learned that the utensil we referred to as a "spider" was a frying pan or skillet, and the "cookies" were actually pancakes. My dad didn't enjoy loaf bread, which he referred to as "wasp nest." He wanted biscuits or cornbread.

Ma taught me many skills including how to apply wallpaper. There is a skill in applying wallpaper with the designs flowing without revealing a seam on the wall. When Viola's cousin Joyce Watson and her husband Lewis built their new home many years ago, I wallpapered their entire home.

All of the skills taught by my mother have served me well throughout my life. By the time I was thirty years old, I had a wife and six children, so my wife appreciated those skills. I cooked, ironed clothes (especially my starched military uniforms), wallpapered rooms, and also made dresses and other outfits for my wife and girls. I went to Montgomery Wards or Sears Roebuck and purchased patterns, material, buttons, and other accessories and proceeded to sew outfits. In addition, in my opinion, I changed and washed as many or more diapers than Viola. In other words, I have never had an issue with distinguishing between so-called wife and husband duties in the home.

Ma understood John 14:6, where Jesus answered, "I am the way and the truth and the life. No one comes to the Father except through me." At the age of twelve, my parents directed me to sit on the Moaner's Bench. Each year in August there was a weeklong church revival with a guest preacher. Every kid between ten and eighteen years of age who had not publicly accepted Jesus as their Lord and Savior was required to spend the week sitting on the Moaner's Bench.

There was preaching, praying, and singing from seven in the evening until midnight or later each night. The older men got directly in your face and prayed feverishly, encouraging you to accept Jesus. Whenever the moaner felt the unction to surrender their life to Jesus, they stood and confessed that to the congregation. Often, the Spirit compelled them to shout and/or run around the room. Some kids sat year after year and didn't get up. The Spirit came upon me on Thursday night of my second year on the Moaner's Bench, and Jesus has been my best everything since.

As a Methodist, my baptism was by sprinklings. Some thirteen years later, I received baptism by submersion at a Baptist church service in Germany in 1965.

My mother also valued education. Thanks to my Grandma Maggie "Peggie" Satchell, I learned to read at an early age. Grandma kept me fully supplied with books and magazines (more about that later). There was no television in the house, consequently, I read everything I could get my hands on. I never learned phonics, so I read and spelled from memory. To this day, I'm a poor speller. Even so, Ma put me in school at the age of five, and I managed to skip a grade later. My parents never missed a school activity, especially if I had a part in a play, etc.

Ma valued hard work and responsibility. I remember getting out of bed in the morning before sunrise and going to the potato field across the road from our house. Someone on a tractor pulled the machine to unearth the potatoes. When the sun came up so we could see the potatoes on the ground, we bagged those vegetables until seven in the morning. Then we returned to the house, washed our face and hands, and waited for the school bus which was driven by no-nonsense Mr. Clarence Joyner (smile).

Often we didn't change our clothes before getting on the bus. Of course, in those days, it wasn't unusual to have holes in the soles of your shoes. We merely put cardboard in the shoes and continued to wear them. We had a pair of school shoes, play or work shoes, and church shoes. In the summer, we were barefoot most of the time.

We weren't allowed to miss school unless we were near death. If you contacted a bad cold, Ma simply rubbed Vick's salve on your chest and covered your chest with a warm towel. Plus, you took a dose of 666 Cold Preparation, Sassafras root tea, drops of coal oil in a spoonful of sugar, and/or the nasty tasting Castor oil. A little baking soda took care of stomachaches, Argo starch for diarrhea, and Castor oil for constipation.

Since we ran around barefoot, we had to be aware of stepping on rusty items for fear of lockjaw, today known as Tetanus. Grandma Elenora gave us various herbal teas. It must have worked because we're all still living. I don't remember visiting a doctor for sickness until I was perhaps twelve years old and injured myself. There was a home remedy for nearly every illness.

Ma never spoke to me in a demeaning manner. She chastised me, sent me to the woods to get a switch, whipped me, and instructed my father to give me a second whipping when he arrived home from work. There was no such thing as "time out." I felt like it was all done in love. In other words, it didn't hurt my self-esteem. I was never called stupid or told I would never amount to anything.

That reminds me of Proverbs 13:24. "Whoever spares the rod hates their children, but the one who loves their children is careful to discipline them." My mother and father must have really loved me because they didn't spare the rod.

Proverbs 31:27 says, "She watches over the affairs of her household and does not eat the bread of idleness."

Ma ran a tight ship. My father trusted her to take care of our home. Now, I'm only speaking for myself, but while husbands are led to believe that we are the final authority in the house, wives really make the rules, don't they? Can I get an Amen from the husband readers?

Ma used to come into our bedroom in the morning and make up the bed with us in it, so you had no choice but to rise and shine. Another comical event involved the goat we had. On occasions, Ma pumped water at the outdoor pump stand, and the goat chased her. Ma would end up on the pump stand with the goat hollering up at her, "Mag, mag, mag." That was funny because my mom's name was, of course, Maggie.

Ma allowed no alcohol in our house. Dad hid his whiskey bottles under the large washtubs hanging in the detached garage and the trunk of his car. My father and visiting grandfather (Ma's dad) often came out of the garage a little wobbly. My brother Melvin and I sometimes sneaked a swig of Dad's whiskey and replaced what we drank with water. We figured that Dad either didn't notice or didn't complain because supposedly our Mom didn't know it was there.

Ma knew and insisted on the type of environment she wanted in her home. She was a loving daughter to her parents (two miles away) and her parents-in-law (half a mile away). She was also loving to my playmates. However, my playmates knew she would put them to work if they stuck around the house long enough.

Back in the day, we didn't have daycare centers. We had Grandma. When our parents worked, we were cared for by our grandparents who maintained the same structure as our parents. My grandparents didn't hesitate to discipline us when appropriate.

Proverbs 31:28 says, "Her children arise and call her blessed; her husband also, and he praises her."

There was never a doubt in my mind that Ma loved me. She will always be near and dear to my heart. She was a woman of sincere faith and not hypocritical about it. Having a sincere faith doesn't imply perfection, but it does imply knowing God is real. Ma sincerely believed in Jesus Christ as our Lord and Savior. She spent time in His Word and prayer. I can't think of one instance when Ma's character was questioned in my mind. I respected her so much that I never wanted to disappoint her in any way. I did my naughty things but was forever mindful of my love and respect for Ma.

Proverbs 31:29 says, "Many women do noble things, but you surpass them all."

Ma surpassed all my expectations of true love. There's a joke in my family that I was such an ugly baby that when people approached the baby carriage, Ma covered my face and said I was asleep. On top of that, between the ages of five and eleven, I had a serious dental problem with too many permanent teeth in the front of my mouth. In other words, I was not a pretty sight, but I always felt Ma's love.

Beginning in 1980, Dad, my siblings and I, plus others, noticed Ma easily choked while eating and drinking. She was sixty-two years old at the time.

Ma and Dad often traveled from their home on the Eastern Shore to visit me in Hampton and Melvin in Virginia Beach. When they visited, Mom enjoyed going to the local shopping malls. It was during one of those trips to Military Circle Mall in Norfolk, Virginia, that Melvin's wife, Leona, noticed Ma slurring her speech. Ma also complained of not feeling well, to the point of having to sit on a bench in the mall before proceeding to the car in the parking lot.

Leona was teaching at W. H. Taylor Elementary in Norfolk at the time. Many of the students' parents were doctors. Parent Alice Johnson was the wife of Dr. Johnson, MD. Leona decided to talk to her about Ma to see if she could offer a suggestion for help.

After a discussion with her husband, Alice made an appointment for Ma with Dr. Pellegrino, a noted Norfolk Neurologist with EVMS and Norfolk General Hospital. Ma, Dad, Leona and I met with Dr. Pellegrino. After the initial diagnosis and further evaluations, he concluded that Ma had ALS (Amyotrophic Lateral Sclerosis), commonly known as Lou Gehrig's disease.

Even after Ma was stricken with this disease and eventually couldn't speak, she simply patted me with her hands to let me know she loved me. I still tap my children and remind them those are "love taps."

Proverbs 31:30 says, "Charm is deceptive, and beauty is fleeting; but a woman who fears the LORD is to be praised."

Ma was a sweet, loving, kind, warm, God-fearing woman. While parents should be the primary agents for teaching our children God's Word, we should also pray for Godly mentors for our children. Apostle Paul was a mentor to Timothy. We must not be so jealous as to think we are the only ones who can influence our children. We should pray for Godly teachers, youth workers, elders, pastors, and other men and women of God to influence our children for righteousness. My mother trusted true believers.

The patriarch of the Allen family, the late William Allen, who was the Sunday school superintendent at our church for many years was a good example. In fact, I served as Assistant Sunday School Superintendent under Mr. Allen. I was probably about thirteen years old at the time. I also remember being the captain of the church youth group.

The main way Ma taught me to love and serve God was through God's Word. The best thing she instilled in me from an early age was the importance of reading, studying, memorizing, and obeying God's word. Being human, I have not always followed that practice.

Paul told Timothy, his protégé, in 2 Timothy 1:5, "I am reminded of your sincere faith, which first lived in your grandmother Lois and in your mother Eunice and, I am persuaded, now lives in you also."

That's the same way I feel about my grandmother Peggie, my grandmother Elenora, and my mother Maggie. The faith they demonstrated and lived every day now resides in me. Let me end this litany by saying that one of the greatest blessings is to have a Godly mother, and one of the greatest gifts a woman can give her children is to be a Godly mother.

Ma resided on the Eastern Shore until her death in 1983 at the age of sixty-five.

At our mother's home-going service, I read the following:

A Tribute to Our Mother

All mothers are special, but we, the children of Clifton and Maggie Collins, have been truly blessed. First, we have a father who continues to be kind, considerate, and loving. Secondly, we were blessed to have had a mother who was the driving force behind every success we have ever enjoyed.

I am up here today because our mother would want it this way. She was a proud, very proud mother with the strength of an elephant, the patience of Job, the kindness of Jesus, and the love of God. We want to share with you our mother as we knew her.

First, she taught us decency and about the love of God and His son Jesus. She was kind and treated everybody as Jesus taught us. Also, our mother taught us the value of self-reliance through sacrifice and hard work. Although God blessed us with a father who always provided for the family, we had to share in the responsibilities early. We had to sew, cook, scrub floors, wash clothes, work in factories, pick beans, and perform many other tasks to help the family.

Secondly, our mother provided us inspiration to achieve. She worked many long days so we could stay in school. We are thankful for that. Many mornings, we followed her to the fields before the sun came up only to be ordered by her to go to school. That motherly concern, love, and struggle put all five of us through college and allowed us the opportunity to live productive lives.

Our mother also taught us thoughtfulness and love for other people. Many of you sitting here today have been touched by her love and concern for you. She loved you as a friend, she loved those of you who were our playmates, and she especially loved to show kindness to the older friends who needed company or a ride to the grocery store.

Our mother was a very affectionate person. Even until the end, she wrote notes of affection and love to us and our friends, for she could not speak.

Lastly, our mother placed a little bell in our conscience which goes off every time we are about to do something of which she would not approve. That bell was put there through our love and respect for our mother.

In summary, our mom was a beautiful mother. She would want us to say thanks to each of you who have come from far and near to be with us today. May God bless each of you and guide you safely home.

Thank you!!!!

~ Melvin ~ Delores ~ Clifton ~ Lafayette ~ Barbara ~

Mother's Family

My mother was the youngest of five sisters and two brothers. All seven siblings are now deceased. Aunt Mildred Fisher is missing from the picture below; however, Aunt Mildred is in the wedding picture in chapter three.

Emma Bryant, Mary Ellen Blackwell, Maggie Collins, James Satchell, and Edna Wescott, circa 1975

Once out of high school, all of her siblings headed north to Philadelphia or New York City except for Mildred and Earl. Aunt Mildred and her husband Holland Fisher lived in Accomack, Virginia, about thirty miles north of our home in Eastville. Uncle Earl built a home next door to his parents and resided there until his move to Richmond, Virginia, twenty-five or thirty years later.

Uncle Earl Satchell and wife, Minerva Upshur, circa 1955

My Siblings

Melvin Collins, Delores Thornton, Clifton Collins Sr, Lafayette Collins, Barbara Eure, picture taken in Poughkeepsie, New York, at Delores's retirement celebration, 2008

Currently, I have four living siblings, Melvin Randolph, Delores Elizabeth Thornton, Barbara Ann Eure, and Lafayette Anthony Collins. Our brother William James Collins was born on November 7, 1942, but died at two months on January 11, 1943. Records indicate that William died of malnutrition. There weren't many conversations about him in the home. Apparently, he couldn't tolerate breast milk from Ma nor cow's milk. Similac and other baby formulas were not available in 1943. Later, my sister Delores had the same problem, but a milk substitute had become available by then.

William's grave is located in a graveyard belonging to our church, Bethel African Methodist Episcopal, Eastville, Virginia, near the intersection of old Route 13 and Old Town Road, across from the former location of my elementary school. The graveyard was not maintained and is completely overgrown. I doubt if anyone's grave can be identified at this time.

Despite their many challenges, Dad and Ma managed to send all five of their surviving children to college directly out of high school. That appeared to be very abnormal on the Eastern Shore among Black or White families. I wasn't aware of their true struggle until going through their personal effects after death and seeing many bank loans.

Basically, our parents had at least one kid in college over a twenty-year period from 1956 to 1975. Over the years, I always marveled at how our parents supported all of us through college, not really appreciating that it covered an extended period with basically no break in time; it was amazing. Later, my father and mother were honored as "Parents of Year" by a local church for that achievement. Many of our schoolmates were stuck on the farm for life.

I graduated from Virginia State University in 1960 with a major in mathematics followed by a military and federal civil service career. After twenty-one years, I retired as a lieutenant colonel from the U.S. Army in 1981 and, nineteen years later, retired as an Operations Research/ Systems Analyst with the federal government in 2001.

Melvin graduated from Virginia State University in 1963 with a major in business administration and retired from a career in federal civil service as a Job Corps Regional Director in 2002.

Delores graduated from Virginia Union University in 1968 with a major in biology followed by a career in social work and civil service. She retired as a warden with the New York State Department of Correctional Services in 2008.

Barbara graduated from the University of Maryland Eastern Shore in 1970 with a major in art education followed by a career as an art educator and owner of four arts and crafts stores. She continues to teach and create exceptional works of art. Her home and gallery have been featured in the Winston-Salem Living Magazine.

Lafayette graduated from Norfolk State University in 1975 with a major in business administration followed by a career in the military and secondary education. He retired as a major from the U.S. Army in 1996, and retired from secondary education and real estate in 2012.

Early Church

I was raised as a member of the Bethel African Methodist Episcopal (AME) church in Eastville, Virginia. Bethel AME church is listed in the National Register of Historic Places for its "distinctive characteristics of architecture/construction." Also, the church is in the *Guinness Book of Records* as having eighty-one beautiful stained glass windows. Some of the church history is found in a book by Frances Bibbins Latimer, *Landmarks, Black Historic Sites on the Eastern Shore of Virginia*.

Bethel African Methodist Episcopal Church, Eastville, Virginia, circa 2000

History has it that Bethel AME Church began in 1866 and is the oldest church in Northampton County. The original structure was lost to fire, and the present building was constructed in 1901.

It's a unique house of worship with the main sanctuary and balcony on the second and third levels, which were accessible only by stairs. Its high cathedral ceiling and numerous stain glass windows are absolutely beautiful to behold.

When I was growing up, it was unheard of to do anything disrespectful while in the sanctuary. When I entered, I didn't even have gum in my mouth, and God help me if I did anything mischievous. We had been taught to revere God, especially in the sanctuary.

Many of the church members are handicapped and require the use of wheelchairs. In the past, they participated in church services by viewing a television screen on the first level or were physically lifted up the stairs to the second-level sanctuary. Even more significant were the countless pallbearers who had to struggle carrying heavy caskets up the winding flights of stairs.

The need to assist entry to the second-floor sanctuary was essential. Years earlier, there were plenty of strong young men attending church. Assisting the handicapped parishioners and carrying heavy caskets up the winding flights of stairways were not as big of an issue. Today, farming is done primarily by machines, and there aren't many young men on the area farms and/or attending church.

During our annual Memorial Day family get-together weekend in 2007, my sister Delores, standing before the church, was led by the Holy Spirit to promise the congregation that upon her retirement in 2008, she was going to help fund the installation of an elevator for easy access to the sanctuary. Standing with her, I promised to have her back, and she and I became major donors.

With the vision of Reverend Timothy W. Johnson and the Godly calling placed on all members and friends, the 148-year-old church experienced a milestone in 2011 when a Liftavator was installed.

The church members worked hard to raise funds by sponsoring seafood dinners, bake sales, yard sales, sandwich sales, and a dinner theater. Donations were solicited from businesses, friends, and former members. As many local families, including the Collins, celebrated reunions, they made donations as well. The Liftavator has been a blessing for the church members and the community. Visitors and members requiring mobility assistance can fellowship in the sanctuary due to increased access. Morticians have also been able to provide bereavement services more reverently. The cost was $136,000, and under the leadership and guidance of Reverend Horace B. Cross, the project was paid off in 2016. Hallelujah!

Collins/Satchell family attending Bethel AME Church in 2008

Chapter 4

My Life Journey as a Youth

I was born near the little town of Eastville on the Eastern Shore of Virginia two years before the beginning of World War II. The Eastern Shore is the common name used to refer to the Delmarva Peninsula. When I was growing up, Eastville was popular for having a debtors' prison, drugstore, bank, post office, and two service stations.

The original state Highway 13 used to run past Herman's Beer Garden, Bethel AME Church, and through the small town of Eastville, Virginia, which had one blinking traffic light. With the advent of the interstate highway system, the current state Highway 13 now bypasses those places.

With the large Navy presence in Norfolk, a common sight was sailors traveling to the Eastern Shore by ferry and then hitchhiking rides north to their destination. They were seen with their thumbs out for miles along Highway 13.

I was told Ma gave birth to me in an upstairs bedroom of her parents' home, tended by the very popular midwife Serena Harmon. During those days, virtually all Black babies were delivered in the home by Black midwives. Initially, my parents lived in a little red house belonging to a White farmer named Heggee James. I remember very little about living in that house.

I do remember the death of my two-month-old brother, William, when I was three years old and an occasion of looking out of the window to see my father walking across the field toward the house with a sack of groceries over his shoulder. I have no idea why those two events have stuck with me throughout my life. I guess it epitomizes the life struggles endured by my parents raising a family in the 1940s and 50s.

Before my fifth birthday, my parents purchased a one-story, two-bedroom house one mile from where I was born. My grandfather Robert Satchell and uncles James and Earl Satchell helped my father convert that four-room house into a two-story three-bedroom house with seven rooms.

Imagine viewing the front of a one-story house; extend the right side out four feet allowing for a stairway in the middle of the house. Then, raise the roof to convert the one-story home into a two-story home. When they finished, there was no evidence of the old structure.

Witnessing this event as a youth convinced me of the skill level displayed by my grandfather, my father, and uncles Earl and James. While most non-college-educated Black men on the Shore were sharecroppers or farm laborers, men in my mother and father's families were skilled tradesmen.

Eastville, Virginia, is the county seat of Northampton County. The courthouse in Eastville was built in 1690 and claims to have the oldest continuous court records in the United States, uninterrupted since 1632. Because the Chesapeake Bay saved the Delmarva Peninsula from experiencing the same type of Civil War battles waged in Richmond, Yorktown, and other mainland areas, the Northampton County court records were not destroyed. To visit the Eastville Courthouse and view the old documents is a special experience.

By the time I was five years old, I could read any material available. I credit mostly my paternal grandmother Peggie for my ability to read early. She worked as a maid on one of the passenger/auto ferry ships (Pocahontas) traversing the Chesapeake Bay from Cape Charles to Little Creek, Virginia, near Norfolk, Virginia. The water trip took two to three hours, and each time the passengers debarked, my grandmother cleaned the lounge area. She worked two days on and two days off. Every time she came home, she presented me with a bag full of discarded magazines, newspapers, and books. Having no TV or electronic devices to occupy my time, I read as much as time allowed.

The first memorable book I received for Christmas was a collection of fables with stories like *The Three Little Pigs, Jack and the Beanstalk, Little Red Riding Hood and the Big Bad Wolf,* plus *Goldilocks and the Three Bears.* That book was like a pot of gold to me. Seventy-five years later, I can still picture the giant climbing the beanstalk and the three bears looking at Goldilocks.

Cousin Kenneth Collins (April 14, 1938 – February 18, 2003), Melvin Collins, Cousin Thomas Collins, Clifton Collins, circa 1947

This picture shows our cousins Kenneth Jr. and Thomas, sons of Dad's brother Kenneth, with my brother Melvin and me. You can probably tell that their attire was in a little better shape than ours. They were city boys visiting from New York. Looking at this picture, I was quite a sight with those big ears and an abnormally large head for my skinny body.

I was not wearing glasses in this picture for fear of breaking them while playing. Melvin's and my clothes were always tattered, and our shoe soles often had a hole in them. For a while, country kids had no idea of the living conditions in the city, but it always appeared that the city visitors had the best of everything—cars, clothes, etc. Little did we know that some of those pretty cars were rented. Plus, when we visited their homes, their conditions were not much better than ours.

In fact, when visiting my Aunt Helen in North Philly, my father had to drive around the block several times before finding a parking spot near her front door. If he parked around the corner, out of sight of her apartment, there was a high probability that his car would be vandalized. When we visited our aunts Edna, Emma, and Mary Ellen, who all had homes in West Philly, there didn't appear to have been as much concern about crime and vandalism.

I was a hard sleeper and often dreamed that I had to urinate. In my dream, I got out of bed, walked downstairs, went outside away from the house, and began to urinate. Well, that woke me up because I was wetting the bed and my poor brother Melvin. Of course, we stayed in the bed for the remainder of the night because it was too cold to get up. I wet the bed until I was twelve or thirteen years old, so I needed at least a birdbath quite often.

Every Saturday, we took a bath whether we needed it or not (smile). We used the outdoor pump to put about five inches of water into a large washtub. The tub was placed on the coal/wood potbelly stove to get the water warm. My brother and I took turns bathing in that tub. When my oldest sister, Delores, came along, she bathed first, followed by Melvin and me, in the same water. Later, my sister Barbara participated in the ritual. Lafayette was only four years old when I left for college. He wasn't required to participate. He was probably too young.

My childhood is filled with good memories. There were always fun things to occupy our time. I remember the domino games, particularly watching the adults play. My father got very excited and slammed the dominos down hard on the table. If you didn't own a dining room table with numerous dents in the tabletop resulting from dominoes being slammed down, you were missing the fun. Pitty Pat was also a very popular and simple card game that anyone could play. My grandma Peggie had a Chinese Checkers game board that I never did master. The regular Checkers game was also very popular.

Growing up Black

I grew up with the threat of being lynched for being in the wrong place at the wrong time. If you take a moment to do an internet search on the history of lynchings in the United States, you'll note the great number of lynching in the nineteenth and twentieth centuries. Predominantly in the southern states, the victims were Blacks and Whites attempting to helped Blacks. The threat of being lynched certainly terrorized me. It appeared that no one cared or ever paid the price for lynching a Black person. The last reported lynching took place in Alabama in 1981. Unlike previous instances, that lynching of Michael Donald by Ku Klux Klan members was successfully prosecuted. To me, the killing of George Floyd in 2020 is a modern day lynching. The House of Representatives has put forth many anti-lynching bills, but finally, the Emmett Till Antilynching Act bill was signed by President Biden on March 29, 2022.

There were also "sundown communities" where any nonresident Black person must leave before sundown or expect trouble. There were two communities near Hampton, Virginia, in the 1970s that still had that reputation.

Jean Isley was a Jewish lady who owned a small one-room store and a separate two-story house about a hundred yards up the road from our house. Ms. Jean often asked me to cut her grass, scrub floors, bring in wood and coal, and do many other tasks. When I completed a task, she paid me with a dollar or so, or with a slice of baloney and cheese, and a honeybun. Her sister lived in the same house, and she always sneaked and gave me a little extra change. Not only that, her sister saved the Sunday paper for me so I could read the comics.

She had a granddaughter about our age. I was constantly reminded by my parents and grandparents to not get caught in the bushes with our little White girl playmate.

What was happening to people of color throughout America caused me to live a cautious life, always being cognizant of my behavior. If you were suspected of looking at or associating with a White woman, you were subject to being lynched.

I was only fifteen years old when fourteen years old Emmett Till was lynched in Mississippi in 1955. He was a Black boy from Detroit accused of flirting with a White woman. During the trial, a Black witness identified two White men as the perpetrators. For a Black person to publicly accuse a White person of committing a crime was extremely unusual. The men were found innocent by an all-White male jury. At that time, Blacks and women could not serve on the jury. Once Emmett Till's body was found, his mother chose to have an open casket funeral so attendees could view his mutilated remains. As a Black teenager, that event in the news had a great impact on my view of justice or lack thereof in the United States.

Just being deemed by a White man as arrogant was enough to get a

Black person in trouble. Can you imagine having to look down when in the presence of a White man? If you looked him in the eye, you were considered to be "uppity" or "insolent." Sadly, the situation is not much better today. Racists and bigots are getting bolder by the day. Could you have imagined five years ago that several fully armed men would be standing at the entrance to a state capital chamber? More about this subject later.

It's been a challenge to live in America as a Black man. I can't even imagine how life has been for other disenfranchised people around the world in a nondemocratic society. Unless you have been the victim of discrimination, you have no idea how it feels.

For instance, when I traveled with my parents or grandparents in the 1940s and 50s as a toddler and teenager, Paul's Drugstore was five miles south of Eastville in Cheriton, Virginia. That was the main stop for the Trailway and Greyhound buses passing through enroute north to Pocomoke, Maryland, and south to Norfolk, Virginia. The drugstore served food and had a sitting area. Black customers could approach the counter, state their order, pay, and receive their order but were not allowed to walk a few feet to sit in the sitting area. We had to take our order outside the drugstore to eat.

From 1956 through 1960 while in college, I experienced similar racial discrimination when traveling by bus from Virginia State College, Petersburg, Virginia. The bus terminal waiting areas were designated "For Whites Only" and "Colored Waiting Room." Once on the bus, we were expected to sit behind the "Colored" line. Enroute on Route 460, the bus stopped at a restaurant for a rest stop. The White passengers went into the restaurant to make purchases and use the bathroom, while the Black passengers were required to use the outhouse in the rear of the restaurant. If we wanted food, we had to approach a window in the rear of the place and receive our order. Persons who haven't endured this type of humiliation tend to not understand.

In the twentieth century, Black people were referred to as "Colored," "Negro," "African American," and currently the most accepted term is "Black." In fact, as a youngster in the 1950s, being called Black was an offensive term. Stokely Carmichael popularized the phrase "Black Power" in 1966. Also in 1968, four months following the assassination of Martin Luther King Jr., James Brown came out with the song, "I'm Black and I'm Proud." It became a major hit and more and more Black people began to embrace the term "Black" as being positive.

In my young days, most businesses that treated Blacks with a bit of dignity were owned by Jewish people. Money or no money, we always got service and credit if requested. Every Saturday, my family drove nine miles south to shop in Cape Charles, Virginia. That was the biggest shopping area in the county. The towns of Nassawaddox and Exmore, Virginia, had little shopping areas, but no other place topped Cape Charles. There was a five and dime store, drug store, clothing store, and shoe store owned by Jews where we could shop. There was always good food sold in Cape Charles. A Black gentleman nicknamed "Do-Tell" served the best softshell crab sandwiches on the Eastern Shore.

Once in Cape Charles, Ma gave us an allowance. When we had accomplished whatever Ma had directed, she allowed us to roam the Five-and-Dime and other stores. Typically, I purchased a large icy drink, box or bag of popcorn, bag of salted peanuts, one or two comic books, ammo for my BB-rifle or caps for my cap pistol, and a large cone of butter pecan ice cream. Then I returned to the car to enjoy my ice cream cone, popcorn, and drink. I can't forget the box of Cracker Jacks with the prize inside, and sometimes even animal cookies. I always saved the comic book and peanuts for my Sunday morning ritual. Early Sunday morning, I awoke and enjoyed my peanuts and comic book before getting out of bed to eat breakfast and attend Sunday School.

Christmas Experience

When I was growing up, Christmas was always a festive time. Melvin and I headed out into the woods early in the morning for the sole purpose of finding the perfect Christmas tree for our home. We walked through woods (the forest) for hours, until we had found the right tree. Then, we cut and dragged the tree to the nearest opening where my dad could retrieve it with his truck. We then walked back to the house and directed Dad to the pickup point. To my knowledge, owners of the wooded areas often had the area posted against hunting without permission, however, they didn't complain about someone harvesting a Christmas tree.

On the night before Christmas, we left a slice of cake and a soft drink out for Santa. Once in bed, we listened intently for the sound of Santa coming down the chimney. Lord forbid if we dared to open our eyes because Santa would put pepper in our eyes. Every bump we heard was Santa coming, dropping off our presents, eating the snack, going back up the chimney, and taking off in his sleigh.

Early Christmas morning, we ran downstairs and searched for our presents. Typically, we found a small paper bag with an apple, an orange, perhaps ten pieces of Christmas candy, and a few shelled nuts. Our toy was perhaps a paper cap gun. As Melvin and I got older, we received a BB-gun, the one requiring the cocking motion. One of our friends received an air-pump BB-gun. The velocity of his BB was much faster and more deadly.

I remember one time receiving a yellow toy dump truck. Needless to say, I filled and dumped dirt all over the yard. To this day, I love big equipment, particularly construction equipment. When I am driving and see a bulldozer, grader, or another piece of construction equipment being used, I nearly run off the highway. I also love to see tractor-trailer trucks that have been beautifully decked-out with decorative lights.

At Christmas time, we always received one set of clothes—shirt, pants, and perhaps a sweater. That was our Christmas, and we were as happy and thankful as we could be. Believe it or not, we were considered privileged children. Many others received less for Christmas.

Elementary School Experience

Every summer as the school year approached, Grandma Peggie took Melvin and me to Norfolk to shop for school clothes. We took the ferry across from Cape Charles to Little Creek and rode a Trailway bus to Norfolk. We walked through the Selden Market and Arcade to reach the Stein Men's Store. Once there, Grandma Peggie bought us shirts, pants, coats, shoes, and anything else we needed for school. She was overly generous and a true blessing.

In fact, looking at the wedding pictures of when I married my first wife, Melvin and I are wearing identical overcoats. I'm sure Grandma Peggie bought them.

Because I could read and my birthday was in November, I was allowed to begin school at age five. At that time, elementary grade levels were "primer," followed by grades one through seven. High school was eight through eleven.

During my entire elementary, high school, and college education, all my teachers and fellow students were Black. My formal education began at Eastville Elementary School in Eastville, Virginia, where there were four teachers. It was a typical four-room school built in 1939 to serve the Black populace. Each room had a pot-belly wood/coal stove as the only source of heat. There were approximately twenty-four students divided among two grades in each room.

Mrs. Vivian Wright was a robust lady who lived less than a mile from our home. She taught primer and first grade. She was a rather large lady who you didn't want to upset if you could help it. Soon after I started school, I requested to sit in the front row. I suppose Mrs. Wright thought I was eager to learn, but it was because I had difficulty reading the blackboard. She and my parents finally realized I needed glasses when I was five or six. I've been wearing glasses ever since.

It wasn't unusual for Mrs. Wright to drop by the house to inform Ma of my progress or lack thereof. Truthfully, I didn't get in trouble in her classroom. I could surely read well, knew my multiplication table, and probably looked like a little nerd with my glasses on (smile).

Once I was promoted to the second grade and moved to Mrs. Jean Whirl's classroom, I quickly learned she was an even more no-nonsense teacher. She noticed that I was completing all of my second-grade assignments, plus, since I was idle, I was also completing the assignments given to her third-grade students on the other side of the room. She soon moved me from the second-grade side of the room to the third-grade side.

The only physical punishment I can remember receiving in elementary school was administered by Mrs. Whirl. She had stepped out of the classroom, and my classmates and I were talking and playing loudly. Upon her return to the room, she rapped every one of us across the opened hand with a black leather strap. Needless to say, we didn't repeat that behavior.

On to Miss Alice Brinkley's classroom for the fourth and fifth grade. I was about eight years old, and Miss Brinkley had recently been hired to teach at our school. She was twenty-three years old, had recently graduated from college, and looked young and beautiful to an eight-year-old child (me).

Miss Brinkley didn't tolerate any foolishness in the classroom. Because I got into a fisticuff with Shirley Gray, a female classmate, after school while waiting for the bus, Miss Brinkley directed that while my classmates were outside playing during the school day recess period, I had to sweep the classroom wooden floor for several weeks. When I was growing up in the 1940s, boys did not hit girls. That was a no, no. Needless to say, I never wanted to get into a fisticuff with any other girl (smile).

I still have my fourth- and fifth-grade report cards administered by Miss Brinkley. At that time, student performance was reflected by three levels, O-Outstanding, S-Satisfactory, and U-Unsatisfactory, four times during the school year. My grades were predominately Satisfactory until the third rating period of the fifth grade when they all were rated as Outstanding. Arithmetic grades were always the exception. Arithmetic was rated Outstanding throughout the school year on every elementary report card I currently have.

My Fourth Grade Class, circa 1948: 1-Ruth Simpkins, 2-Dorothy Sample, 3-Shirley Gray, 4-Eyvind Harris, 5-James Sample, 6-Clifton Collins, 7-Mary Brown, and 8-Miss Brinkley

This is a picture of my fourth-grade class. On the front row are three of my cousins, Ruth Simpkins number 1, Dorothy Sample number 2, and Eyvind Harris number 4. Number 3 is Shirley Gray, my fighting buddy, who probably got in more licks than I did in our fight and received no punishment. Number 5 is James Otis Sample, my lifelong friend until his death in 1998. Number 7 is Mary Brown, the best speller in the class. I am number 6 and number 8 is Miss Brinkley.

I continued to excel in school, and Miss Brinkley always chose me for the lead part in various plays. For instance, I can distinctly remember being in the Christmas play as the shoemaker. There was a folding wall between Miss Brinkley's and Mrs. Smith's rooms which could be opened to form an auditorium. Miss Brinkley's room had a raised stage. With the center wall folded, it served as a decent-sized auditorium. My parents never missed a performance.

Then on to Mrs. Alice Smith's sixth- and seventh-grade classroom. Mrs. Smith also served as the school principal; she was the wife of Mr. William

H. (Bear) Smith, the principal of Northampton County High School. I don't have my sixth-grade report card, but my seventh-grade report card reflects all Outstanding grades. One thing comes to mind that might have caused the drastic improvement in my grades.

At the age of five or six, my permanent teeth replaced my four top baby teeth in the front with two fused double teeth, plus one single tooth behind each of the fused ones. In other words, there were six teeth where there should have been only four. Between the ages of six and eleven years old, I was always self-conscious of my ugly smile. Those teeth were pulled and replaced by a partial when I was in the sixth grade at the age of eleven. Perhaps, the improvement in my self-esteem brought about the improvement in my grades. More about my dental experiences later.

One exercise I remember very vividly was being required to go to the blackboard (no whiteboard back then) with only a piece of chalk to draw a map of the United States with the outline of each state, its name, and capital.

While I was in the sixth grade, education officials visited the school and administered tests to all classes. My parents were informed I had scored at the tenth-grade level. I often wonder how my life would have changed if I had been moved to an even higher grade level.

As it were, I experienced some difficulty in my social life, as well as in sports, because I was two years younger than my classmates. I think that social development is as important as educational development.

When I graduated from elementary school, I was chosen to be the valedictorian of my class and had to write my speech. On the day of the graduation program, I practiced my speech to the audience of Miss Brinkley and Mrs. Smith. I froze and couldn't get a word out. I'll never forget Miss Brinkley simply reassuring me she understood and I would be okay that evening during the program. With my parents and others sitting in the audience that evening, I did fine.

I will never forget my very first sentence. "My friends, to me falls the saddest part of this day of pleasure. I must leave this great school and wonderful teachers." Miss Brinkley attended my family's annual Memorial Day Cookout until her death in 2016. I will never forget her.

Stupid Things Kids Do

Because my parents worked, I spent a lot of time at my maternal grandparents' home. Children often do stupid activities without regard for the danger of their activities.

As kids, we made slingshots that could hurl a missile (such as a pebble) two hundred or more yards. John, Leroy, Melvin, and I harvested several ears of horse corn one day, shucked it, and used the kernels as missiles. Horse corn is very hard versus sweet corn which is rather soft. The dangerous part of this story is that we were shooting at each other in the upstairs bedroom when we were supposed to be going to sleep.

There were two double beds in the room. Using blankets and pillows as shields, we covered the beds and floor with corn. It's a wonder that no one lost an eye that night. Grandma Elenora was not a happy camper the next morning. She fussed and made us clean up but no whipping. Grandpa never disciplined or dealt with us; he always told Grandma to take care of the kids.

There are events in your youth that make a major impact on your life forever. One day, probably at age ten or eleven, I was walking around with my BB-gun in the woods behind my grandparents Robert and Elenora's house looking for sassafras root for my grandmother to make sassafras tea. I spotted a small bird high up in a tall pine tree. I pointed my BB-gun and made every attempt to hit that bird.

I finally struck him, and he began spiraling towards the ground and fell at my feet. After a few jerky movements, he was dead. Well, after that, I never pointed a gun at another animal.

My father was an avid rabbit, squirrel, and raccoon hunter, but he never asked and I never requested to join his hunting party.

Other than my brother Melvin and cousins John and Leroy, my best friends were Calvin Sample, Clarence Reid, and Samuel Satchell. Clarence lived a couple of miles away but our buddies Calvin and Sam lived nearby and hung with my brother Melvin and me to do mischievous things.

Across a field and through the woods was a farmer who grew the best watermelons on the Eastern Shore. We sneaked to the edge of the woods adjacent to the watermelon patch, confiscated a couple of watermelons, and returned to the cover of the woods. There, we burst them open and ate the best part, the heart of the melon. The farmer John Collins (not a relative, according to Dad) learned of our antics and sat on his porch and waited with a shotgun. Fortunately, he never caught me or my friends, but he did catch another young man, and Dr. Allen had to pick buckshot out of his butt.

High School Experience

I attended the Northampton County High School in Machipongo, Virginia. The teachers, administrators, and all students were Black. The one situation that perplexed me the most was the apparent lack of federal and local support at Northampton County High School, as compared to support provided to the all-White Northampton High School, five miles down the highway. More about this disparity later.

A typical school day began by being awakened by Ma, using the pee-pot, getting dressed, and going downstairs. For breakfast, I got a bowl of cornflakes and filled the bowl with milk if we had it; if not, I used water. Then I ate a biscuit or roll with molasses and waited for the bus.

Most of the time, all of the bus seats were taken by the time it got to me, and I stood for the three-mile trip to elementary school or the five-mile trip to high school.

Academically, I did well enough in high school to graduate fourth in my class. I was never one to study that much, but God had gifted me to survive and keep my head above water. Old report cards reflect I was never a great fan of language and history, however, I always did well in mathematics and science.

Mr. Albert B. Whitehead and Mrs. Mary Collins were my favorite high school mathematics instructors. I've always loved mathematics because it's an exact science. Two plus two has always equaled four. Personal opinions don't count. I still have a philosophy paper I wrote in 1959 during my junior year in college and received a D because my "philosophy" was not acceptable to the professor.

I began my senior year in high school at the age of fifteen. My girlfriend Virginia Rogers was one grade behind me. Although we were a couple for about three years and considered a forever duo, we gradually parted ways after I left for college.

Clifton Edward Collins Sr. in high school, circa 1954

As you get older, there are some events in your past life that you fondly remember. Perhaps, one of my fondest memories of high school was attending the Junior/Senior Prom. As a high school junior, I wanted to attend the prom, however, Virginia was a sophomore and was not eligible to attend. There was a young lady in my class who had medical issues, and no one had asked her to the prom. I decided to ask her, and she happily accepted. I always cherished that event as one of the most gratifying memories of my life. I was glad I made her happy. Virginia and I attended the prom the following year.

In the "La Circle Francais" picture below, I'm the third student in the second row from the right, caught with my hand up participating in the French class. Over the years, I never really used my knowledge of French.

LA CIRCLE FRANCAIS

French Class: Clifton Collins is third student in second row from the right (with hand raised), 1956

As a math major in college, I was required to take German, which I later used while stationed in Germany in the military. During the 1950s, German mathematicians such as Albert Einstein were very highly regarded. Math concepts have not changed for centuries, and many were written in languages other than English. Plus, there was a German professor on campus (smile). Had I pursued a doctorate degree in math, I'm sure I would have been required to research documents written in German, Russian, French, etc.

Here I am the President of Section A of my junior class (the fourth student from the right in the back row). Miss McQuaige was my homeroom and French teacher.

JUNIOR A CLASS

VICE-PRESIDENT

BUS. MGR.

SGT. AT ARMS

SECRETARY

PRESIDENT

Otha Turner   Harold Drummond   M. Bailey   C. Collins

Dorothy Mapp

TREASURER

Maryetta Weeks

We, the Junior "A" Class entered the Northampton County High School on September 2, 1954, with high hearts and renewed ambition. We are progressing rapidly under the guidance of our Homeroom Teacher, Miss McQuaige, and are cooperating the best we know how in our many school activities. Our aim for the year was to excel in all that we undertook. We feel assured that with the guidance of our teachers and our principal we can not fail.

As the Seniors reach the ladder of success, we hope they will leave a light burning, so that we may follow.

HOME ROOM TEACHER

Miss M. E. McQuaige

There is no doubt in my mind that my first wife Viola and our six children can sing better than I, but there I am in my high school chorus . . . trying. I'm the middle student in the back row.

The Northampton County High School Chorus. Clifton Collins is the middle student in the back row; 1955-56 school year

I continued to do well in school while participating on the football and track teams. I was okay at football and pretty good at track (shotput, javelin, and discus) but was never skilled enough to make the basketball or baseball teams. Because I had started school at age five and skipped a year, I was normally one or two years younger than my classmates. Well, when you're in your teens, one or two years make a big difference in terms of maturity as well as size.

Throughout my elementary and high school years, I had a strong yearning to play sports. After all, my cousins John and Leroy Wescott had always paired with Melvin and me to play baseball and football every day. John and Melvin were great athletes, but Leroy was an exceptional athlete. My biggest hindrance was my eyesight.

Wearing glasses since I was five or six, I couldn't see well enough to fully participate in sports. I never heard of contact lenses. Can you imagine being the catcher and not being able to see the ball coming at you very well? Thankfully, our ball was normally a tennis or rubber ball. They didn't hurt that much when it missed the glove (smile). Even while playing high school football, especially at night, I couldn't see well enough to know where the football was. I merely tackled anyone nearby.

Perhaps, one of the most famous athletics to attend my high school was Johnny "Happy" Sample, who transferred to Overbrook High School in Philadelphia two years before the picture below was taken. Johnny's real name was John B. Sample Jr. He was a redhead kid who excelled at every sport. He was captain of the football, baseball, track, and basketball teams in the same year. In football, he was the punter, kicker, and quarterback. On the track team, he ran the 100, 200, and 440-yard races. In baseball, he played third base and batted number four in the lineup. In basketball, he was the top scorer. It was said he could run the 100-yard dash in ten seconds while wearing the complete football uniform, pads and all.

He went on to Maryland State College and later played with the Baltimore Colts and other professional teams. Johnny is the only professional football player with a National Football League, American Football League, and Super Bowl championship ring. He wrote a book, *Confessions of a Dirty Ball Player*. Johnny died in 2005 at the age of sixty-seven.

Northampton County High School, 1955-56 Football Team.
Clifton Collins is number 15 in the back row.

Our coach took our team to Maryland State College to a football game. Johnny Sample and Stan Jones, a current resident of Newport News, Virginia, were on the team. Stan and I talk about those days even today. While visiting Maryland State, my high school teammates and I were given a tour of the locker room. A vivid memory was seeing Sherman Plunkett, a tackle on the Maryland State College football team putting on his uniform. I had never seen a man that big. His legs looked like large tree trunks. The internet states he weighed 290 lbs., but he looked like the Jolly Green Giant to me. He also played for the Baltimore Colts, San Diego Chargers, and the New York Jets.

Of course, my high school didn't have a stadium with lights to use at night. On one occasion, we traveled to Norfolk, Virginia, to play against

Booker T. Washington High School in a lighted stadium. The coach allowed me to play a few plays at the tackle position. I surely couldn't exactly keep up with the football, but I will always cherish the memory of being in the game. We lost the game, and I remember being ushered onto the bus immediately afterward because the coach had gotten wind of visiting teams in the past being ambushed by local students and fans. We were not.

Each year, in preparation for our football season, we waited for the farmer to harvest his crop and smooth the field as best he could because that farmland served as our football field. On the other hand, the all-White Northampton High School, five miles down the road, had a stadium with bleachers and lights for night games. We were never allowed to use that venue. I always thought of how unfair things were.

My participation on the track team was a little better because I threw the discus, javelin, and shotput. Poor eyesight was not a great hindrance. I don't recall ever winning first place, however, participation and being on trips away from home were the highlights for me.

Although I discovered later that my elementary and high school curricula were not as comprehensive as found at many other schools in places like Richmond, Virginia, my teachers were fantastic. They were all college graduates from Black colleges and universities. Under the circumstances, they did a superb job. Examples of the challenges faced by my elementary teachers included the requirement to teach two different grade levels of students the complete variety of subjects (math, English, history, etc.) in the same room, with no partition between the classes.

For instance, when I was in the second grade, the student at the desk next to me was in the third grade. I found myself giving attention to what was being taught to the third graders and raising my hand to answer the questions being posed to them. That is the reason, Mrs. Whirl decided to simply move me over to the third grade in the middle of the school year. Basically, my eight classes of elementary education were taught in seven years in four classrooms.

At least in high school, teachers were assigned to teach only in one specific area such as English, history, or mathematics. The books used throughout my elementary and high school were always hand-me-downs from the all-White school. Not only were there names of prior users but there were often missing or marked up pages.

I cherish the experiences under the tutelage and guidance of my teachers. They taught us to respect and honor and reinforced the discipline rendered at home. I never witnessed any student disrespecting a teacher or administrator. Any minor infraction resulted in punishment at school followed by further punishment at home. The teachers deeply cared, and we learned the material offered.

The major information omitted from my education, even through college, was knowledge of White against Black violence. My textbooks only discussed Black against White violence. I was constantly reminded of events such as Nat Turner slave rebellion. But, I was not informed of Whites against Blacks events such as the Tulsa, Oklahoma, and Rosewood, Florida, race massacres.

Basically the history we were taught was from books written by White authors. Much of what I know today about Black history was learned after I turned forty and later. In elementary and high school, I knew about famous Black people such as Booker T. Washington and George Washington Carver but very little about achievements by other Black people. My parents simply taught us about the Ku Klux Klan and that was as a cautionary measure to keep us safe.

A good example of how the education of Blacks has been misleading is the 1921 event in Tulsa, Oklahoma. I recently learned—at eighty-one years old—about the 1921 Tulsa race massacre which had been portrayed in the textbooks as the Tulsa race riot. Because a nineteen-year-old, Black, shoeshine boy was accused of assaulting a seventeen-year-old, White, female, elevator operator, mobs of White people killed more than three hundred Black people and injured hundreds more. Prior to this massacre, Blacks in Tulsa prospered, and Tulsa was deemed to have the Black Wall Street.

In school, we didn't learn about the significant participation of Blacks in the Civil War, World War I, and other conflicts. In fact, I was not knowledgeable of the lynching of Black veterans after World War I for merely having on the uniform until I was gathering information for this project on the subject of lynching, and this is 2020. Research of this type of information is informative, overwhelming, but also very depressing.

I highly recommend the reading of the 1852 speech by Frederick Douglass, *What to the Slave is the Fourth of July?* made on the seventy-sixth anniversary of the signing of the Declaration of Independence. He addressed the continuing enslavement of millions of people while celebrating independence of the nation. I was in awe of how elegant he spoke, having been a former slave with limited opportunity for education. I wish we had been exposed to that type of speech in lieu of or along with speeches such as the 1864 Gettysburg Address by Abraham Lincoln.

Steps to begin the integration of truthful African American History into the school curriculum took place after the racial uprisings in the 1960s.

DOROTHY BURGESS

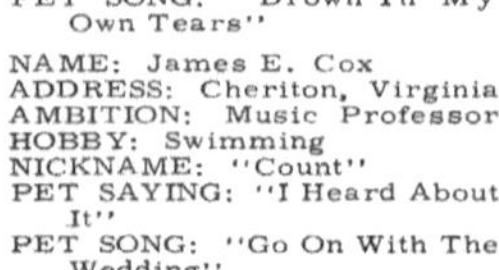

GLORIA COLLINS

JAMES COX

GEORGE CUSTIS

CLIFTON COLLINS

SALLIE COLLINS

BERTIE CRAWFORD

MARY CUSTIS

NAME: Dorothy M. Burgess
ADDRESS: Box 33, Cape Charles
AMBITION: Nurse
HOBBY: Cooking
NICKNAME: "Dot"
PET SAYING: "Lawdy Miss Clawdy"
PET SONG: "You Got The River Of Jordan To Cross"

NAME: Clifton E. Collins, Jr.
ADDRESS: Box 271, Eastville
AMBITION: Mathematician
HOBBY: Playing Football
NICKNAME: "Clip"
PET SAYING: "How About It"
PET SONG: "Bo Diddley"

NAME: Gloria C. Collins
ADDRESS: 524 Peach Street, Cape Charles, Virginia
AMBITION: Nurse
HOBBY: Reading
NICKNAME: "Peaches"
PET SAYING: "Oh! Boy"
PET SONG: "Great Pretender"

NAME: Sallie A. Collins
ADDRESS: Bridgetown, Va.
HOBBY: Softball
PET SAYING: "Are You Kidding"
PET SONG: "Drown In My Own Tears"

NAME: James E. Cox
ADDRESS: Cheriton, Virginia
AMBITION: Music Professor
HOBBY: Swimming
NICKNAME: "Count"
PET SAYING: "I Heard About It"
PET SONG: "Go On With The Wedding"

NAME: Bertie A. Crawford
ADDRESS: Box 102, Eastville
AMBITION: Interior Decorator
HOBBY: Reading
NICKNAME: "Ruth"
PET SAYING: "Without A Cause"
PET SONG: "I Wouldn't Mind Dying"

NAME: George Custis
ADDRESS: Eastville Station
AMBITION: Auto Mechanic
HOBBY: Football & Baseball
NICKNAME: "Jabo"
PET SAYING: "Hey Now"
PET SONG: "Steam Boat"

NAME: Mary E. Custis
ADDRESS: Seaview, Virginia
AMBITION: Nurse
HOBBY: Studying Science
PET SAYING: "Don't Be Foolish"
PET SONG: "Rock & Roll Waltz"
NICKNAME: "Squirt"

My classmates cited me for "Best Personality," "Most Cooperative," and "Most Versatile." (Page from my high school yearbook)

For a time period in the 1960s, Black students were allowed to attend the all-White Northampton High School, however, the Black and White students were physically separated. Northampton County High School ceased operations as an all-Black high school with the 1970 class. Until 2008, the facility served as a racial integrated junior high school and middle school for all Northampton County students. It's now a school administrative facility.

Youth Employment

Farm work could be divided between planting and harvesting. Most of the planting was accomplished by local workers. The majority of the harvesting was accomplished by migrant workers. We wrongfully referred to the migrants as "Florida people." Each year, they arrived by buses and trucks, were housed in migrant camps, and moved from one large farm area to another, from the southern tip of the Delmarva Peninsula to the north, as far as New Jersey.

I began to work on the local farms at an early age, probably six years old, until I left for college at the age of sixteen. Around the first of May each year, we harvested strawberries early in the morning. There was dew on the plants, which tended to cause our fingertips to split and crack. Gloves were almost a must, but they slowed you down. We were paid ten cents per strawberry basket.

During the summer break, we worked ten hours every day during the week and five hours on Saturdays for twenty-five to thirty-five cents an hour. The work was varied. For example, we weeded crops with a hoe, harvested (i.e. picked) tomatoes, beans, and peppers one-by-one by hand, picked up white and sweet potatoes, manually harvested sweet corn, spinach, and cabbages for twenty-five cents an hour, and drove tractors and trucks for fifty cents per hour.

Often, we were required to irrigate the crops. Once the irrigation pipes were connected and irrigation of an area was completed, we had to manually disconnect and lift the eight-inch by thirty-foot aluminum water pipes over our heads, walk them across twenty or more rows, and reconnect them, time and time again until the entire farm had been irrigated. Today those pipes are mounted on wheels and mechanically positioned to irrigate the entire farm, perhaps by one operator.

When semi-tractor-trailer trucks arrived on the farm to be loaded with produce (i.e., crates of sweetcorn), Melvin and I offered to load the truck for the drivers for fifteen dollars. They gladly accepted that deal. The trucks arrived with a pile of chipped ice on the floor of the trailer. Melvin and I put a layer of ice on top of each row as we stacked the crates. Fifteen dollars for two to three hours of work was a good hustle for us.

The major farmers we worked for were Harold Wescoat and Roy Acuff. They owned most of the farmland near our home. Harold Wescoat managed to get a special driver's license for me to drive farm equipment, which included farm trucks, at thirteen years old. Viewing my thirteen-year-old grandsons, I can't picture them driving a farm truck loaded with hundreds of baskets of tomatoes or bags of potatoes down state Highway 13.

Today, most crops are harvested by large machines. In the 1940s, '50s, and '60s, most crops were harvested by hand. It went something like this. If we were harvesting white potatoes, the tractor drivers pulled a piece of equipment (potato digger) that uprooted the potatoes to be picked up by hand and put into a peck size basket. Two of those filled baskets were dumped into a potato sack, weighing approximately fifty pounds. Looking down a finished row, hundreds of these sacks sat ready to be loaded onto the flatbed truck.

When I was the truck driver, I simply steered the truck into the row, shifted to extra-low gear, got out of the truck, and allowed it to creep down the row driverless. I then loaded the sacks onto the truck flatbed on the driver's side while someone else loaded on the passenger side. A third individual was on the flatbed stacking the sacks. As the truck approached the end of the row, I jumped in and turned the truck onto the next row and repeated the loading process. We switched sides when it was safe to do so because we held onto the truck with one hand and loaded the sacks with the other hand. This switch allowed me to conduct my driver duties and at the same time balance out muscle use.

Once the truck was completely loaded with perhaps 300 or more sacks, I drove eight to ten miles to the potato-grader facility. Upon arrival, it was my responsibility to pour every sack into a harper where an ever-moving belt conveyed the potatoes into the building. Inside, several workers (normally ladies) threw out the unwanted potatoes and the good potatoes were conveyed into one-hundred-pound sacks. The unwanted potatoes became hog feed, and the one-hundred-pound sacks were loaded onto tractor-trailer trucks for shipment to upstate markets.

During the planting season, tomato (red, green, or yellow) and other plants were placed in the ground by two people sitting backward on a low moving planter machine pulled by a tractor. At the right speed, the two individuals could place a plant every ten to twelve inches in the trench made by the planter machine. The machine was ingenious. Not only did it make the trench, but it also spurted water and covered the root of the placed plant.

Later, as the plants took root and began to grow, we used a tractor to cultivate along the plant rows to destroy weeds and promote growth by increasing soil aeration and water infiltration. In other words, the apparatus on the tractor broke up the soil around the plants. When the plants got too big to cultivate without harming them, as many as ten or more individuals took a row and used a hoe to cut the weeds from around the growing plant. We worked in that hot sun from seven a.m. until noon, took an hour for lunch, and then worked from one until six p.m. Every hour or so, a truck appeared to bring us drinking water—one pail and one dipper from which we all drank.

When harvest time came, we picked tomatoes by the double peck at ten cents each. A double-peck is equivalent to one-half bushel or what we called a tomato basket. I picked one hundred baskets of red tomatoes in one day. Ten dollars was big money in those days. Cabbages were the worst things to harvest because they held water and caused our fingers to crack and hurt. Normally, the harvest took place late in the fall, therefore, it was cool in the mornings when we harvested cabbages. There was always a barrel with burning rubber tires in the area to warm our hands.

Hard work or not, one of the fondest memories I have was the group of us singing as we worked. Frankie Lymon and The Teenagers was our favorite group. *Why Do Fools Fall in Love* was a great song for us to harmonize.

As mentioned earlier, when I was growing up, virtually every kind of vegetable and fruit was grown on the Eastern Shore—white potatoes, sweet potatoes (including the famous Hayman variety), snap beans, butter beans, cabbage, tomatoes, sweet corn, spinach, turnip greens, peppers, and strawberries. Even if someone didn't own a garden, the farmers released the fields after their harvesting period, as the Bible speaks of in the Book of Leviticus 19:9-10 and 23:22. One could glean, can, and preserve lots of vegetables and fruits that lasted through the winter. Couple that with the slaughter of a pig during the Christmas season, and there was sufficient food to feed the family for the year.

When the weather got cold in late December, the men in the neighborhood gathered at each other's house to slaughter a pig. For instance, at our house, Dad used a 22-caliber rifle to shoot a pig through the forehead. The throat was cut to drain and capture the blood, and then the pig was hung by the hind legs. The hair was removed using scalding hot water and clamshells. Once cleaned, the pig was gutted and every part was saved, i.e., guts, heart, kidneys, tail, feet, liver, and testicles (known as Rocky Mountain Oysters).

The guts were later used to make the best sausage you have ever eaten. The meat was cut into chunks and placed into the smokehouse to be salted down for preservation. The feet and ears were pickled. The belly fat was cut up to make lard and cracklings.

This same ritual was repeated at everyone's home until the neighborhood had their pork for the winter. Beef was obtained by families pairing up to purchase halves of slaughtered cows. Of course, we always had chickens running around.

White and sweet potatoes were placed in the wooded area near our house. We dug a shallow hole in the ground and filled it with pine needles or straw. The pine needles or straw kept the potatoes from touching the ground and sprouting roots trying to reach groundwater. After filling the hole, we covered the potatoes with other pine needles or straw for the winter. Whenever Ma needed potatoes, we simply went to that mound, gathered what she needed, and recovered the pile.

There was talk of government assistance to provide butter, cheese, flour, powdered milk, cornmeal, peanut butter, and canned fruit to the needy, but apparently, we didn't qualify.

One of the main jobs I had as a teenager was to cut the yard of Mr. Ernest Drummond, the owner of the drugstore in Eastville. Pushing a gasoline lawnmower, it took in excess of eight hours to complete the job. It's difficult for me to imagine pushing a lawnmower for eight hours in the hot summer heat, but I did. The lawnmower had bicycle-sized rear wheels; therefore, it wasn't that difficult to push. It was the hot sun and being alone for eight hours that got to me.

My father was a man of many talents, especially when it came to earning money. He contracted to paint houses and then assigned me and my brother to do the job. To this day, I'm afraid to climb a ladder. Those country homes often had many gables, requiring the ladder to rest at precarious angles. But, my father instructed us to have the job completed by the end of his workday, and that is exactly what we did.

Entertainment

Growing up on the Eastern Shore was wonderful for a kid. Every five to ten miles, there was a small town—Cape Charles, Cheapside, Cheriton, Eastville, Reid Town, Treherneville, Nassawaddox, Exmore, etc. Each town had a church, baseball team, beer garden, and/or store. The towns of Treherneville, Exmore, and Cape Charles even had a movie theater. The theaters in Exmore and Cape Charles were patronized by everyone; Black patrons had to sit in the balcony. The Treherneville Theater was owned and patronized by Blacks only.

Every Sunday after church, there was a baseball game in one of the towns. You had to be an excellent athlete to play on those teams. Every little town had the semblance of a baseball diamond. Nothing fancy, and perhaps the outfield sloped down a little in left or right field, but it was a diamond.

In my youth, there were lots of folks in every household, primarily because there was farm work available. The towns had no problem fielding a complete baseball team with excellent talent. Many of the players were super talented. I never got the opportunity to play a real baseball game with the Eastville team. I wasn't old enough or talented enough. My entrepreneur father didn't play ball either, but he purchased large bags of raw peanuts, roasted them, filled up small paper bags, and peddled those peanuts at the games, along with sodas.

We played all kinds of games to keep ourselves entertained. We stayed outside all day. It wasn't unusual for us to roam the woods for hours, finding running streams of water, playing with tadpoles and frogs, climbing trees, sucking the nectar of honeysuckle, and eating blueberries, etc.

Dad told us of a galvanized pipe that he and his brother Kenneth had driven into the side of a hill to tap into spring water. We found that pipe, and the wonderful spring water was still running. To my knowledge, it's probably still running water, although we may not be able to find it due to the forestry overgrowth.

Our other activities included flying homemade kites, shooting marbles, riding bikes around and around through obstacles, rolling hoops, pulling packers, and playing baseball, dodgeball, hopscotch, hide-and-go-seek, and knuckles. You probably recognized every activity except pulling packers and playing knuckles.

Packers was another one of our conceived games. As Ma emptied various size cans that had tops, we saved them and filled them with sand and rocks, anything to generate noise when rolled. Running wire through the cans, we hooked them one behind the other, from biggest to smallest, and tied string to the front one allowing us to pull the packers as we ran around the yard. If you refer back to my childhood picture with my brother and cousins in Chapter 4, take note of the cans on the ground. My cousin Kenneth is holding the string attached to that series of cans we called packers.

Knuckles was a game we conceived where we used a clamshell to carve three bowl-shaped holes about three feet apart. The aim was to shoot your marble from one hole into the next hole. If you missed, then you had to place your fist in front of the missed hole and allow your opponent to shoot his marble as hard as possible from the first hole to strike your knuckles. Believe me, those marbles hurt.

In our youth, we made several crude toys to entertain ourselves. Every boy had a homemade slingshot. First, we found a small Y-shaped tree limb about four inches wide and six inches long. Then, we tied a twelve-inch strip of rubber which had been salvaged from a bike or car inner-tube to each tip of the "Y." The part to hold the small pebble or rock projectile was the tongue from a discarded leather pair of shoes. We often shot at birds and other animals, or even each other sometimes.

Melvin and I never owned a new or more than one operational bike at any given time. From time to time, Dad found parts of bikes at the dump, and we managed to piece together a ridable one. Unlike today's tires, our tires had inner tubes that needed patching often. When the tires were no longer usable, we simply rode on the rims.

Melvin and I rode double on the single bike with Melvin pedaling while sitting on the crossbar and me pedaling while sitting on the seat. Due to our double horsepower with our feet on the same pedals, we could normally beat others in a bike race (smile). In the meantime, our cousins John and Leroy were living with our maternal grandparents. They were given brand new bikes by their mother, Edna, who lived in Philadelphia. They were beautiful red and white JC Higgins bikes that even had spring shock absorbers on the front.

Being mindful of the importance of enjoying our youth, several years ago, my wife and I purchased bikes on sale and took them to the Eastern Shore to donate to children chosen by the local social worker.

It was indeed a luxury to own a baseball glove. We played pickup games in the middle of the asphalt road, for we weren't allowed to play in the planted farm area and the yard was too small because of flowers and trees. We played with a tennis or rubber ball and a broom handle as our bat. Hitting the small ball coming at you at perhaps eighty miles per hour with the skinny boom handle took skill. Ma often yelled a warning to get out of the road because a known drunk was heading our way. Several gentlemen fell into that category.

One day, John and Leroy joined Melvin and me to play a pick-up baseball game. I fell and hit my elbow on the pavement, leaving a quarter-coin size hole in my elbow such that the white ligaments were showing. My grandmother took me to Dr. James Allen's office where he approached me with a curved needle and thread to sew up the wound. I took off and ran out the back door of the office. After much coaxing and threats from my grandmother, I returned to the office because he promised not to use that needle on me. He proceeded to pack the wound and wrap it. I still have the scar on my elbow.

During my early years, smoking was entertaining. We made pipes out of corn husks and stuffed them with cigarette stumps discarded by our fathers or others. If we couldn't find cigarette stumps, we used dried corn silk. Of course, the nearby store owner up the road wouldn't sell us cigarettes. Grownups could buy single cigarettes or the whole pack. I began smoking earnestly when I entered college at the age of sixteen. My brother Melvin worked for Phillip Morris Tobacco Company while attending Virginia State. After his arrival on campus during my junior year, I never ran out of cigarettes.

I tried cigars for a very short time, perhaps a month. They were too strong to inhale. Then I tried pipes which I enjoyed, but soon a little white patch appeared inside my jaw in April 1972. The doctor suggested that continued use of the pipe might create cancer in my mouth, so I settled for cigarettes. By the time I was thirty-six, I smoked two to three packs of cigarettes a day. There were no restrictions on where you could smoke. But, I had four boys from six to fifteen years old, and I didn't want them to smoke. So, I made up my mind to quit.

Well, it was extremely difficult. I tried the patch, chewing gum, and every other deterrent, including bumming off of other people. I even gave someone five dollars at the beginning of the week to allow me to bum off of them. During those days, an entire ten-pack carton was ten dollars. I tried quitting by taking only three cigarettes a day to work, one with morning coffee, one after lunch, and one enroute home. Finally, I determined that the only way to quit was to quit cold turkey. Taking it hour by hour and day by day, with a few setbacks, I eventually quit completely. I craved cigarettes probably for a year afterward. Sinusitis had been a constant ailment for many years, but once I quit smoking, that problem ultimately went away.

When I was growing up on the Eastern Shore, we participated in the annual May Day activities at the Weirwood Fairgrounds on the first Thursday of May. May Day was one day when all Northampton County Black school children dressed in white t-shirts and blue jeans and spent a full day at the fairgrounds. We participated in Dance around a Maypole, track competition, balloon toss, and other games. Of course, all kinds of food, snow cones, ice cream, and candy were available.

In August, there was a week-long Fair in Weirwood, Virginia, followed by another week in Tasley, Virginia, twenty miles farther north. It seems that every Black family within one hundred miles attended the two fairs every year. Although many of the venues were manned by White personnel, the attendees were 99 percent Black.

The fair was held all week; however, the big day was Thursday when there was harness horse racing. My father loved the races. The horses raced at a fast trot pulling a two-wheeled cart called a sulky, occupied by a driver. Dad got absolutely excited because he knew most of the race drivers and always favored one of them.

Various games were available that included the accuracy of a thrown ball, coins tossed in a bottle, bingo, merry-go-round, bumper cars, etc., but there were also X-rated shows that we boys tried to view through cracks in the tents, called Hoochie Coochie Shows. Recently, I did an internet search for Hoochie Coochie Shows, and let me tell you, those shows at the fairs were a lot more risqué than what I saw on Google.

Ma packed food for the family. Arriving at the fairground around ten in the morning, Ma instructed us to meet at the car at three p.m. to eat. With the allowance our parents provided, we couldn't afford the food sold at the fair venues. Besides, our mother's food was much better.

Most enjoyable was walking around the fairgrounds hand and hand with my girlfriend. That was an ideal time to show off.

Youth Dating

My brother Melvin and I double-dated and had to be home by half-past midnight. On Friday nights, we frequented Club 13, one-mile south of Eastville; Herman's Club, one-mile north of Eastville; the Bud Edmonds' Club, five miles north in Nassawaddox; and Little Herman's Club about twenty miles north in Little Boston, Virginia. There was lots of dancing, great food, and beer drinking. The smoke in those clubs could be cut with a knife.

My father allowed us to use the family car on Friday and Sunday evenings but never on Saturday, due to an increased probability of drunk drivers on the roads. The car was always very stylish, and it was a dream to drive. One car I fondly remember was the '55 green Ford Fairlane. It was the sharpest car in the area.

Clifton Collins leaning on the 1957 Mercury family car, and brother Lafayette Collins can be seen in the background, circa 1959.

Later, Dad purchased a beautiful 1957 black and white Mercury and allowed Melvin and me to drive it on dating activities. A major dating activity I loved was taking my girlfriend to the drive-in theater in Exmore, Virginia. The popcorn was the best, and you could certainly enjoy the movie and intimacy with your sweetheart. Remember, we didn't have a television, so theaters, particularly drive-in theaters, were very popular.

Most of the beer joints in Northampton County were required by law to close at midnight, and our parents expected us to be home thirty minutes later. Often we violated the curfew and drove thirty miles north to the Kinsey Seaside Club in Accomack County where they served the best fried chicken sandwiches. Or we drove to the Little Boston, Virginia area to the Little Herman's Club. Apparently, those two establishments in Accomack County didn't have to close at midnight.

The clubs had unfinished wooden floors that appeared to have been sprayed with motor oil to minimize the dust, particularly in the dance area. At the bar, you could purchase beer (if you were over 18), soft drinks, snacks, potato chips, and chicken or fish sandwiches. Whiskey, gin, and other liquor were not authorized for sale. Most men kept those drinks in the trunk of their cars. The law didn't allow open alcohol bottles to be in the passenger area of vehicles. It wasn't unusual for friends who met on the backroads to stop, chat, and share alcoholic drinks from the trunks of their vehicles.

During those days, the weapon of choice was a pocketknife. Seldom were people shot, but we often heard of people being stabbed or cut. Fights were almost always between grown men who had too much to drink or during an argument over the affections of a female. There were not many teenage fights.

Many of the entertainers who later became widely famous came by the clubs. Those were the days of Chuck Berry, Fats Domino, Little Richard, Ray Charles, Sam Cooke, and James Brown. One entertainer I vividly remember was Bill Doggett, the Honky Tonk Man. I saw him perform at a club in Delaware when I was working my summer job at the chicken plant.

Ignorance of certain aspects of life can often be a blessing. As far as I was concerned, I had a great young life.

Dental Care Experience

Dental care was a challenge on the Eastern Shore. First, as a youngster, I wasn't taken to a dentist unless I had a toothache, often, not until an abscess had appeared. I remember having a toothache one night, and my parents felt that a medical doctor in Eastville was my only hope. Well, the doctor didn't have dental tools, not even a dental-type chair. He sat me in an armless chair and proceeded to use whatever tools he had to extract that tooth. Of course, my father was extremely strong and held my head and body still throughout the procedure.

There was a dentist located in Cape Charles, Virginia, a nine-mile drive away. Those visits were absolutely terrifying. First of all, the dentist had a drinking problem; he had the alcohol bottle sitting on the same tray as his dental tools. When I had work done, my father and any other gentleman available had to physically hold me down for the dental procedure.

As mentioned earlier, the six teeth located between my eye-teeth were extracted when I was approximately eleven years old, in the seventh grade, by a dentist in Nassawaddox, Virginia. At that time, all six teeth were replaced by a partial, the likes of which I continue to wear today. When the dentist stuck the numbing needle in the roof of my mouth, I thought the world had ended. It was a pain I've never encountered in my entire life again.

To add to my fear of dentists, while I was a student at Virginia State College (now University), the dentist in Petersburg who was contracted to service the students also had a drinking problem. I witnessed him hollering out of his second-floor office window asking a friend to purchase and bring him a bottle of alcohol. Soon, that bottle joined his dental instruments on the tray.

My fear of dentists didn't lessen until I was well into my 30s. While in the military, I requested and received Valium-type medication prior to all dental visits. For that reason, I always took my kids to a pediatric dentist where the doctor fully understood the dental treatment of children. Praise the Lord, the results are obvious. Although three of my kids required braces, they all have a blessed dental outcome and history. Moreover, Viola and I were strongly in favor of making fruit available for the kids rather than candy. Having six kids, we called the commissary and requested crates of oranges, apples, pears, and other fruits be held for our later pickup. The kids were given unlimited access to the fruit. They purchased candy whenever they could use their small allowance.

Chapter 5

College Experience

Upon graduation from high school, I received a tuition scholarship from the state of Virginia and academic awards from the Cosmos Club and other organizations on the Eastern Shore. I decided to attend Virginia State College (now University) (VSU) in Petersburg, Virginia. I had considered the University of Virginia but there were only a few or no Black students being accepted in 1956.

I decided to major in mathematics but didn't fare very well. This was primarily due to lack of effort, but also to the lack of several prerequisite high school courses. Many of my freshman mathematics classmates had taken solid geometry, calculus, and trigonometry in their respective high schools. Those courses were not offered at Northampton County High School. The only math courses offered were algebra and basic geometry. Couple that lack of preparation with my immature activities to have a grand old time in college, I failed almost every course in my freshman year. In fact, I was informed by the college officials that I was to sit out the first semester of my sophomore year.

Well, my mother didn't accept that outcome. She was determined to not allow her oldest child to fall through the crack, and I had to set an example of graduating from college for my four younger siblings. She wrote the college and state officials, solicited supportive letters from my high school principal and other prominent people, and managed to not only get me back into college without sitting out a semester but also got my academic scholarship reinstated. Needless to say, she was successful, and the rest is history.

Another factor that may have contributed to my poor performance as a freshman in college was that my roommate had a much different background. He was a Korean War veteran majoring in automotive mechanics. He was probably five years older than I was, and his classes required more hands-on rather than book-study. All we did was smoke, drink alcohol, and visit the female dormitories, especially Byrd Hall, the freshman dormitory.

Every Friday and Saturday night, a disc jockey played music in the basement, and we slow-dragged until we were put out at eleven-thirty at night (smile). Slow dragging is a dance where you simply rub bodies as close as possible. Studying was never on my mind until the night before a test. During those days, I had the gift of a photographic memory wherein I could picture the pages in the textbook as required. That gift normally enabled me to get a passing grade. Of course, I had the infamous slide rule or so-called slipstick in my back pocket at all times. That item impressed the young ladies as an indicator of "smartness" (smile). At that time, the slipstick was our mechanical analog computer. It was used in all of my mathematics, chemistry, and physics classes for doing division, multiplication, logarithmic, and trigonometric functions.

At VSU, every male was required to serve two years in the basic Reserve Officer Training Corps (ROTC) program. Enrollment in the third and fourth year advanced ROTC program was not required. Although I had scholarship funds, I still needed the monthly stipend offered for enrollment in the advanced ROTC program. Consequently, I passed the required exam and entered into the advanced ROTC program which provided that monthly stipend for my junior and senior college years. This decision obligated me to serve for two years on active military duty upon graduation. I had no intention of making a career of the military. I planned to do my two years and go to work for some large company as a mathematician.

I'm sure my parents sacrificed a great deal to get us through school. I chose not to work during the academic year and learned to survive on my scholarship and award monies plus the ROTC stipend beginning in my third year. I was penniless most of the time, but on occasion, I went into town (Petersburg) and earned wages hanging tobacco in the warehouses.

Although my grades were less than desirable, the athletic department advertised for a student to provide math tutoring for athletes. I applied and got the job. Believe it or not, they paid me five dollars per hour to tutor those athletes in the basement of Vawter Hall. That was good money in the 1950s. On the farm, it took me ten hours in the hot sun to earn five dollars.

There is something to be said about immature kids being sent to college with very little supervision. I don't recall any occasion when I was called in by a college professor to discuss my class performance. That was a sharp contrast to my elementary and high school days when I was always receiving some form of counseling. Not only did I not study regularly in college, but I also found many, many other non-class related things to occupy my time.

A typical day included eating three meals every day in the Jones Dining Hall, spending long hours in Foster Hall shooting pool and playing ping pong, visiting the girls' dormitory to stroll with my girlfriend across campus, returning to the dormitory later to escort her to the movies on campus, and lastly, attending the dance in the girls' dormitory basement that evening. Studying? What was that? Oh, I was also on the wrestling and track teams. Those activities required daily practice and team travel to the various campuses in the CIAA conference.

No matter what I did or didn't do, I am the man that I am because of it, and I'm not complaining. I thank my good Lord for keeping me.

Reserve Officer Training Corps (ROTC)

During the summer of 1959, between my junior and senior years at VSU, I attended the ROTC summer camp at Fort Knox, Kentucky. The camp was six weeks long and it was my first experience of being in close living conditions with White people. In the barracks, there were predominately White ROTC cadets from Virginia Military Institute and other college programs all over the country. We were all going through the same difficult and challenging training. I will never forget climbing Agony and Misery Hills with the heavy M-14 rifle and backpacks weighing a "ton." Moreover, the road marches with full military gear were no fun either. Shared hardships tend to make people get along with each other. I didn't witness any racial problems during the six-week camp. I also learned I could compete successfully with people of other races.

Armed with weekend passes, many of the cadets ventured into Louisville and other towns to enjoy the bars, girls, and sights. Those of us who didn't leave the post often visited the post exchange to shop and drink beer. While finishing off cans of beer, we saw how high we could stack empty cans on the table. Needless to say, we were often staggering back to the barracks to be just sick little boys.

Periodically we were required to dress sharply and perform guard duty on the weekends. When your turn came around, there was often a fellow cadet who gladly took your place for the right price. I chose to voluntarily replace fellow cadets every weekend. The key was to get paid and not have to perform the duty. The trick was to have a stiffly starched uniform, spit-shined shoes in a high gloss, a fresh haircut, and memory of the answer to every anticipated question to be asked at the guard mount.

After a shower and shave, I stood on my footlocker to carefully put on my pants without breaking the crease in the pants. Once fully dressed and with my rifle on my shoulder, I walked stiff-legged two blocks to the guard mount. Once in formation with perhaps twenty other cadets, I focused on being chosen as the sharpest and most knowledgeable cadet in the formation. If so, I was chosen as the supernumerary cadet, released from guard duty, and allowed to return to the barracks and count my money.

Joining Kappa Alpha Psi Fraternity Inc., April 18, 1958

In my sophomore year, I was recruited to join a fraternity. I chose to pledge Kappa Alpha Psi Fraternity, Inc., in the spring of 1958. My choice was primarily based on the behavior of fellow students who were members. Their interests, good and not so good, seem to have jelled with my interests. Many of the members were athletes, seemingly very mature, and smart.

There were Kappa men I had known as a youngster on the Eastern Shore such as my cousin James Collins and teachers Charles Monroe, William Sisco, and Calvin Brickhouse. I was also aware that William "Bear" Smith, my high school principal, and several other school officials and teachers on the Eastern Shore had pledged Kappa. Frazier Brickhouse and other upperclassmen on campus from the Eastern Shore were already members of Kappa. I liked how

The Kappa Alpha Psi Shield

those men participated in the community and on campus.

Guys who pledged with me included William Bailey, a friend who had attended high school in Accomack County on the Eastern Shore; George Foster, a physics major from Martinsville, Virginia; and George Arrington, a Korean War veteran from Newport News, Virginia.

Throughout the pledge period, we were always tired due to lack of sleep. We were required to run multiple errands and perform various tasks for the big brothers such as shine their shoes, etc. One day in my civilization class, the teacher called on me to answer a question, and in my stupor, I jumped up and stated loudly, "I'm barbarian number four."

At the end of that three to four-month pledge period, I would have done bodily harm to anyone making any derogatory remark about my fraternity brothers or the fraternity as an organization.

The four of us communicate even today, after more than sixty-five years. With the exception of Foster, we were together to celebrate Arrington's eighty-fifth birthday and my eightieth birthday. Foster was caring for his parents and could not join us.

Kappa Alpha Psi pledges William Bailey, George Foster, George Arrington, and Clifton Collins (the four barbarians) at the Virginia State College, April 1958.

I continue to be a major contributor to the various funding programs at Virginia State University, including the efforts of the Alpha Phi Alumni Chapter of Kappa Alpha Psi and the Class of 1960 (Platinum Level donor).

I haven't been interested in attaining a leadership position within the fraternity, however, I've been keenly interested in financially supporting our youth program, the Kappa League. I also actively participate with the Senior Kappa group and assist in the chapter's tutoring program. At this writing, there are more than one hundred youngsters (mostly males) active in the program, participating in sports, and other life-enhancing activities. Brother Arthur Price has devoted his life to that program for more than thirty years. I truly commend him and his wife, Erma.

Following graduation from college, I was inactive in the fraternity for many years. I couldn't afford to maintain my financial membership. Trying to support a wife and six kids by the time I turned thirty years old was quite a challenge. In my 40s, when I returned to the Virginia area by being assigned to Fort Monroe, I became active with the Newport News chapter of Kappa Alpha Psi and remain affiliated with the consolidated Hampton/Newport News Alumni Chapter today.

Summer Jobs While in College

One of the most memorable periods of my college years occurred during the summer breaks of 1957 and 1958. I will forever be grateful to my cousin Gloria and her husband Hyland Johnson for opening their home to me while I worked at a chicken plant in Millsboro, Delaware. As an immature college kid, they ensured I had a job under Hyland's supervision and provided the adult presence I needed. Gloria and their kids spent most of their summers in Virginia with her parents, Earl and Minerva Satchell. Hyland and I visited Gloria and the family on the Eastern Shore every Saturday after work and return to Delaware on Sunday evening. Of course, I was required to pass my paycheck to my mother during that visit every weekend. She provided me sufficient cash to sustain me during the week. Working at a chicken plant helped a great deal in that area. We ate lots of chicken.

Picture this. Trucks carrying 60,000 live chickens arrived at the plant daily. Hung by the feet and moving on a conveyor line, their heads were cut off, followed by a scalding water bath to remove the feathers, then to workers on both sides of the conveyor line to remove remaining feathers. Flawless chickens were removed from the conveyor and packed in containers with ice for transfer to the packaging department. Chickens with the slightest bruise or flaw were left on the conveyor headed for the cut-up section in the plant. That's where I worked.

My crew stood on an elevated platform with the hanging chickens passing by us at a never stopping rate. Each person was assigned to remove a certain part of the chicken as it passed our position. For instance, I may have had the responsibility to remove the left wing. Cut off parts were thrown into one hundred-gallon tanks located at our feet and filled with icy water.

One summer, Melvin and I went to Wildwood, New Jersey. Melvin had worked in a novelty shop on the boardwalk previously. He had a guaranteed job waiting. I spent two weeks seeking a job and finally gave up and traveled to Philadelphia to stay with my aunt Emma. She was scheduled to report to a job in the Poconos at the Hilltop Hotel. My cousin Leroy and I decided to accompany her and seek employment at the hotel.

We were hired to work in the kitchen. That went along fine for about five to six weeks until Viola, my future wife, traveled from Philadelphia to visit me on a weekend. She was visiting her aunt Edith Jasper for the summer. When Viola's visit came to an end and she was scheduled to return to Philly, I asked my supervisor for a pay raise or I was going to leave the Poconos. Well, as you probably expected, I was on the bus with Viola heading back to Philly. When my mother learned I had quit my job, she was quite upset because I had another semester to complete in school.

Prospect of Federal Civil Service Employment

During my junior year at Virginia State, students were given the opportunity to take the Federal Civil Service Examination. I took the exam in the Foster Hall auditorium with over one hundred students. The exam consisted primarily of mathematics and reading comprehension, and we were required to write a 250-300-word paper on our choice of five subjects. The paper couldn't contain more than three errors (grammar, spelling, punctuation, etc.).

Praise the Lord, I passed the exam that year. In my senior year, I began to get invitations from governmental agencies for job interviews. I was interviewed at the Social Security Office in Petersburg, Virginia, the Army Supply Depot in Richmond, Virginia, and the Army Supply Depot in Philadelphia, Pennsylvania. Needless to say, I couldn't accept any civilian position because I owed Uncle Sam two years of active duty for having taken Advanced ROTC in my junior and senior years at VSU.

Chapter 6

Marriage to Viola Vernell Burrell

During my stay at Virginia State University, female students were not allowed to leave campus except for official matters. In my junior year, a friend Preston Royster persuaded me to travel to Richmond, Virginia, with him to visit his girlfriend Hattie Brandon at her home. Being a horny teenager, I convinced Preston to stop by the home of a young Virginia State University freshman girl I dated on campus. She was at home in Richmond for the weekend. When I met her mother and attempted to take her daughter out on a date, she didn't grant permission, so we left.

Preston and I headed for Hattie's home. When we arrived, she suggested that we visit her good friend Viola Burrell. I was willing and ready. Upon arrival at Viola's, I was immediately struck by Viola's beauty and bubbly personality. Needless to say, I couldn't persuade her to accompany us on a date or to even take Hattie home. I guess she saw the gleam in my eyes.

That was the Wednesday before Thanksgiving in 1959. I traveled home for the Thanksgiving holiday and took a young lady out on Friday night in my father's brand-spanking-new-looking '57 black and white Mercury. After dancing and a few beers at the Bud Edmonds' Club in Nassawaddox, I decided to take the young lady home and went into a curve too fast on that country road. The car managed to jump the ditch and settled ten feet from the wood line. Fortunately, a farmer came by, hooked a chain to the rear end, and pulled the car back onto the pavement. There appeared to have been only minor damage to the right front fender. The car was drivable.

I took my date home and returned to the club and told my brother Melvin what had happened. He convinced me to return to the scene of the accident and contact the police. He said that the insurance company wouldn't repair the car if there was no police report. So, I headed back to the scene after calling the police at a phone booth. When the policeman arrived, I was dressed in my ROTC uniform and on my best behavior. He had me sit in the front passenger seat while he wrote the ticket. I was charged with reckless driving.

When I arrived home, I went upstairs, and of course, Ma was awake. After hearing my story, she woke my father. He simply asked if I was okay and where was the car. Once I told him I was okay and the car was in the yard, he simply said, "I'll check it in the morning," and went back asleep.

Because of the reckless driving charge, I was required to be represented in court by a lawyer. Dad accompanied me also. I was given a six-month suspended sentence and court cost; an amount I can't remember. What I do remember is the fifty dollars charged by my lawyer. In those days, that was two weeks of labor in the fields. My dad made me pay every dime from my only source of income, the ROTC stipend.

Following the Thanksgiving break, I returned to campus on Sunday, November 29, 1959, and called Viola. I had never heard anyone so excited about a telephone call. She said she thought she would never hear from me again. From that day forward, I visited by bus nearly every Saturday or Sunday afternoon. Once I reached the bus station in Richmond, I rode the city buses and debarked within a street block of the house.

Our dating experience was mostly sitting on the sofa looking at television. I didn't have a car, Mr. Jasper didn't volunteer his, so Viola and I merely sat on the sofa, talked, and sneaked a periodic kiss. When ten p.m. rolled around, I said my goodbyes and headed for the bus stand.

Viola worked a secretarial job at Virginia Mutual Insurance Company in Richmond, Virginia. She also had an extremely close relationship with her aunt Hortense Matthews, her mother's sister. She and her husband Emmet Matthews were very kind to us.

In my senior year at Virginia State University, Viola agreed to attend the ROTC ball on campus. It was a joyous occasion, and this is one of my favorite pictures.

Viola Burrell and Clifton Collins at Virginia State University ROTC Ball, 1960.

Viola's mother, Mrs. Addie Jasper, and stepfather, Mr. John Jasper, were very friendly and kind and made me feel truly welcome in their home. Mrs. Jasper was a fantastic cook who appeared to get much, much joy out of people eating a lot. Well, being a teenage college student, I had no problem making her happy. I could really put away some food.

During the warm weather months, Viola and I often took walks in Maymont Park. Mrs. Jasper initially required that we take Viola's little sister Jacqueline (Jackey) with us. Jackey and I now reminisce about her riding on my shoulders.

Viola had graduated from Armstrong High School in Richmond, Virginia in 1955 and proceeded to attend the Smith-Madden Business College in Richmond for two years to earn a degree in Secretarial Science. She took courses in shorthand, accounting, business law, speed reading, business management, business machines, salesmanship, English, typing, and psychology. That's where she met and became lifelong friends with Hattie Brandon, who later married Viola's uncle Thomas Watson. Hattie and Thomas Watson were Teri Watson Barnett's parents.

Viola saved my college career because, for the first time, I made a sincere effort to finish school by studying. I was in my fourth year and too many courses behind to graduate with my class in May 1960. So, during my second semester of senior year, I took eighteen credits, rather than the normal twelve to fifteen. When I returned in the fall, I took an additional eighteen credits to complete my graduation requirements. Believe it or not, twelve of those eighteen credits were in mathematics and physics, my major and minor subjects.

I successfully completed my requirements in early December and got married on December 24, 1960. Our wedding ceremony was held at the home of Reverend Terrell, Viola's pastor. My brother Melvin was the best man and Hattie Brandon was Viola's bridesmaid. In attendance were our parents, siblings, several aunts and uncles, the midwife who assisted my birth, and many others. Reverend Terrell's house was full of many people wishing us love and happiness. The wedding reception was held in a restaurant in the Church Hill section of Richmond.

Viola Collins, Clifton Collins, Hattie Brandon & Melvin Collins, December 24, 1960

Just finishing college, merely twenty-one years old and married, I had NO idea what I had gotten into. No job, nowhere to live, but thank God, our friends Richard and Jean Waller who lived two houses from Viola's mother on Georgia Avenue agreed to let us live with them until February when I was scheduled to enter the Army on active duty.

94

(NOTE: As an aside, on June 13, 2020, I spoke with Richard Waller, the owner of Waller and Company Jewelry in Richmond, Virginia. His establishment was vandalized during the George Floyd's death-inspired protests. He was not discouraged and was in the process of restoring his business.)

Our early days of marriage revealed the dichotomy of our upbringing. I always knew that we were raised differently. I was raised in a home with loving parents and nearby loving grandparents. Her parents had divorced many years earlier, and due to custody battles, Viola spent very little time with her mother. Since preschool, Viola had lived with her father, Clarence Burrell, Grandmother Addie Ewell, Uncle Cales Meekins, and Aunt Fannie Meekins. There was love in her family, but the dynamics were different than how I was raised.

Clifton Collins, Clarence Burrell (Viola's Dad), Addie Jasper (Viola's Mom), Viola Collins, circa 1975

My marriage to Viola lasted forty-one wonderful years until her death in 2002. Along the way, there were many amazing times but also some rough times, as expected when you have six kids in the first ten years of marriage. The rough times centered around trying to support and nurture the kids while living on a less than optimal financial income. The struggle was a blessing in many ways, in that we were in the experience together. We had to depend on each other for love and support. Every effort was made to portray unity in all aspects of family dynamics. Even when we disagreed, the kids never witnessed our disagreement.

I'm very much like my dad. I will smile and talk to a fence post if it talks back. There are no strangers in the world, and I'm as comfortable with the window washer as I am with the company president. Over the years, my personality has gotten me into hot water with not only Viola but also Brenda, my current wife, because they often felt I was being too friendly, especially with the ladies. I must admit that some ladies on the receiving end do misinterpret my friendliness. That is the primary reason that my response to ladies asking about my wife is always, "She is fine, just as sweet as ever. Thanks for asking."

Chapter 7

Beginning of Military Life

Entry into the Military as a Second Lieutenant

As part of my college graduation, I underwent a medical examination at Fort Lee, Virginia, and received my second lieutenant commission. Viola and I left for Fort Sill, Oklahoma, on February 14, 1961, in the 1954 Ford Fairlane I had purchased from my cousin Leroy Wescott. That was a trip to remember. First of all, I was aware of only three routes to get from Virginia to Oklahoma—the northern, central, and southern routes. Each route had challenges. The northern route took us through the snowy hills of the northern states, and February wasn't the best month if you didn't want to deal with snow chains for tires. On one occasion, when we were traveling in Pennsylvania, I had to stop to put on tire chains—not a pleasant task in the midst of a snowstorm.

The central route took us through the mountains of West Virginia, and superhighways weren't in existence yet. Navigating narrow roads in the mountains was interesting. Once, we were traveling along an open highway in Tennessee and the car hood blew up. Praise the Lord, I didn't lose control of the car. I had stopped for gasoline, and in those days, the attendant pumped your gas and checked the oil. Apparently, the hood had not been shut properly.

The southern route took us through the southern states where Blacks were truly not welcome. During those years, the routes took you through every little town, where you had to worry about where to eat, sleep, and get gas. On one trip from Oklahoma to Virginia, our vehicle broke down in

Louisiana on a Friday afternoon. As God would have it, we were taken to a service station directly across from a motel that accepted us for the weekend.

For this first trip, we chose the central route. We traveled day and night. When I got tired of driving, we stopped at a drive-in restaurant, got our food, relocated the car to a remote spot in the parking lot, ate the food, and I rested my head in Viola's lap for a spell. She remained awake to be the lookout until I was ready to drive on. It was almost impossible to find a hotel that would accept Black travelers. I wasn't aware of the Green Book which listed hotels, gas stations, and restaurants that were hospitable to Black visitors. Besides, we weren't rolling in money to afford a hotel.

Three or four days later, we arrived in Lawton, Oklahoma, and I reported to Fort Sill to begin the Field Artillery Officer Orientation Course (February 24 through April 19, 1961). Over our twenty-one years in the military, Viola and I traveled all three routes, and there are many stories to tell.

Viola and I enjoyed forty-one wonderful years of marriage for several reasons. First of all, we both believed in God and His Beloved Son, Jesus Christ.

Second, when we departed from Virginia on that faithful day in February 1961, we were on our own. We had to depend on each other. We didn't feel that mommy and daddy had—or could even afford to have—our back.

Third, Viola didn't hang out with the girls, and I never hung out with the boys. We were always with each other.

Fourth, I danced with another lady once and held her too close for Viola's comfort, so I never slow danced with another lady again.

Fifth, at a friend's house party that first year of marriage, I became intoxicated and didn't remember a lady sitting on my lap. That didn't go over well with Viola. I never allowed myself to become that intoxicated again. Except for an occasional wine, I stopped drinking all alcohol and even beer at the age of about thirty-five. Viola never drank alcohol except for an occasional glass of wine. She never smoked either. She only loved herself some "Cliff," and you better not touch him (smile).

First Home after Marriage

The military has always had a great policy of assigning a sponsor to members when they receive orders to relocate. Our White assigned sponsor contacted us with extremely useful information to settle into military life. Once I reported for duty at Fort Sill, the housing officials informed us there was no available housing on post and provided a list of homes advertised for sale or rent. Our sponsor steered us to the section of Lawton, Oklahoma, occupied by mostly Black families. We finally settled on renting a brand new Jim Walter modular prefabricated home. Although new, I remember that the assembled house left wide cracks in the floor such that we could see ants under the house, and the wind whipped through the cracks in the wall joints.

I soon made the first big mistake in my marriage. I went to a nearby furniture store and bought the necessary appliances and furniture for our new unfurnished home on credit. I was naïve of the exorbitant interest rate on the loan. My second lieutenant base pay was only $221 a month. After rent and utilities, there wasn't much left over to pay the appliance and furniture bill. Plus, it had been confirmed soon after our wedding that Viola was pregnant with our first child, Clifton.

Our baby doctor was located in downtown Lawton, Oklahoma. During a visit to his office, I was in the waiting room when the doctor beckoned me to come into the treatment room. When I arrived at the entrance, all I saw was Viola lying on a gurney with a white sheet up to her neck. Well, my knees buckled, and I had to be revived. There was nothing seriously wrong. The doctor only wanted to discuss a minor surgical procedure to remove a mole that Viola had requested.

This was my firstborn, and I must have sent this picture to every person for whom I had an address. Clifton Jr. was a bundle of joy.

Until I was sixteen years old and started college, I thought I was a "Jr." I learned later that since my father's middle name was Herman, I

US Army Lieutenant Clifton Collins Sr. holding six-month old Clifton Jr. at Fort Sill, Oklahoma, in February 1962.

wasn't really a junior. When my first son, Clifton, was born, I became a senior, and he became a junior. Later in life, I wished I had changed my middle name to Herman to become Clifton Herman Collins Jr., and then my son would now be Clifton Herman Collins III. On the Virginia Eastern Shore where I grew up, my nickname was and continues to be Clip, but I'm known as Cliff elsewhere.

In the next nine years, Viola withstood the natural birth of five additional healthy babies, with me merely sitting in the waiting room on four occasions. I was never invited to witness the births. I don't think I would have survived without passing out, anyway. The twins were born while I was in Vietnam.

Viola and I were blessed with good neighbors, Sergeant Lawrence and Yvonne McMorris; Sergeant Major Willie and Lula Hopkins; Horace and Joyce Billups; and Warrant Officer Harold and Pauline Perkins.

The Hopkins lived across the ditch from us and had a house full of children, perhaps seven or eight. Mrs. Hopkins (Lula) was an excellent cook, and Viola and I accepted many of her invitations to dine with them.

Harold and Pauline Perkins sponsored many house gatherings, and they had a below-the-ground tornado shelter. So, at the hint of a tornado, my family walked the two blocks to their home. The shelter was fully stocked with food, water, first aid kit, and more. In the 1960s, while tornadoes were common in Oklahoma and Kansas, there was no talk of tornados on the east coast of the United States.

After a few months of living in downtown Lawton, Oklahoma, I opened an account at the Security and Trust Bank. At the bank, I met Mr. Jerry Mustain, a kind White gentleman, who handled all of my bank business for several years. No matter where I was in the world, a simple phone call rendered approval of any transaction, including loans. For example, if I wished to purchase a car, Mr. Mustain instructed me to find the vehicle, write the check, and he covered it.

Officer Orientation Course Performance

Upon arrival to the Field Artillery Officer Orientation Course (FAOOC) at Fort Sill, I found myself surrounded by brand new lieutenants from probably every state in America, and many foreign officers. There were very few Black students, probably less than 5 percent. FAOOC consisted of three weeks of common core classes and five weeks of branch-specific instruction.

I soon learned my mathematics skills were very useful. We studied the deployment of artillery howitzers, missiles, as well as nuclear weapons. We were required to compute the effectiveness of the various weapons on the target. Nuclear weaponry computations were quite complicated, and because of my love for mathematics, I loved every minute of it. In fact, I graduated in the top of the class, which was a major reason for my induction into the ROTC Hall of Fame at Virginia State University.

First Unit Assignment

Following my graduation from FAOOC, I remained at Fort Sill and was assigned to Headquarters Battery, Third Observation Battalion, Twenty-sixth Field Artillery for four months. The battalion consisted of a headquarters battery and batteries A, B, and C. While the battalion was commanded by a lieutenant colonel, each lettered battery was commanded by a first lieutenant or captain. Lieutenants were a dime a dozen throughout the battalion. Captain Gordon was the only other Black officer in the battalion, and he commanded C Battery. One fact became very clear to me as the days passed. As a Black lieutenant, I was given responsibility for service activities, the motor pool, supply room, mess hall, and communications. The positions commonly known to be career-enhancing were few and far between. For the first four years, my assignments were centered around being a communications officer, survey officer, radar officer, training officer, motor officer, and supply officer.

My superiors learned I was a pretty good writer. Among my other tasks, I was directed to write several documents to include the standard operating procedures for the battalion, commonly referred to as a SOP. I was also given some of the less desirable tasks.

One task stands out in my memory. While assigned to the unit, a military aircraft with many of our personnel crashed in Yakima, Washington, and the personal effects were returned to my battalion. Guess what officer was assigned to accept, personally inventory, catalog, screen, and ship personal effects of the deceased soldiers to their loved ones. That was a rough task, bringing back memories of going through my uncle's personal effects after he was killed on Pork Chop Hill in Korea some ten years earlier.

I also learned years later that my evaluations were not as excellent as I had been led to believe. During the early 1960s, the Officer Efficiency Reports (OER) were written and submitted to the Military Personnel Center (MPC) in Washington, D.C. without being shown to the officer being evaluated. Whether the White officers were shown their reports prior to submission, I don't know. I know for a fact that I never got to see my evaluations until I traveled to the MPC some five years later.

That's when I learned that the words were okay, but my placement on the personnel pyramid was the killer. At that time, the OER reflected a pyramid with a one-person figure on top for outstanding rating, followed by four people for exceptional, followed by twelve people for superior, etc. If you weren't rated at the top level, your hope for great success in the military was bleak. While I was verbally commended for my performance of duties, the OERs submitted weren't reflective of those verbal evaluations.

There was always the context of keywords. For instance, there is a great difference between, "he is outstanding" versus "he has the potential of being outstanding." Or, "he does an outstanding job" versus "he does an outstanding job with minimum supervision."

In the 1960s, being an officer in the military was looked upon as a big deal. We were considered officers and gentlemen. For any minor infraction, the officer suffered serious consequences. For instance, don't get a speeding ticket, don't bounce a check, don't get caught in any store downtown in the fatigue or work uniform, and don't have a creditor to write your commander for nonpayment.

When I got myself into a financial bind by over-obligating myself with new furniture, I called my mom for help. My parents couldn't honor my request for financial help during that rough period, so I had to look for additional income.

The military has always provided thirty days a year for vacation. To alleviate the financial dilemma, I chose to use my thirty-day vacation to procure a job. I went downtown and learned a new school was being built. I approached the supervisor and procured a job as a bricklayer helper. Because the personal vehicles of military personnel displayed a sticker in the windshield indicating whether the owner was an officer or enlisted person, I parked my vehicle two or more blocks from the worksite to preclude being identified as an officer.

In the 1960s, military officers, being officers and gentlemen, weren't supposed to perform menial jobs. It didn't garner respect if the enlisted soldiers witnessed an officer doing menial jobs. Most important, after that four-week additional income, we were out of a financial bind. I never asked, nor had to ask, my parents again for financial assistance. We learned to live within our means. During those days, companies accepted partial payments. For a period, I sent a note to several creditors stating I would be submitting partial payments for a specific number of months. Anything to preclude harm to my credit or military career.

In our early years of marriage, money was always a little tight. Viola was truly a low-maintenance wife; she didn't demand expensive clothes, jewelry, or other things. We created ways of having low-cost mini vacations. Being in the military helped a lot. For instance, while at Fort Sill, Oklahoma, we drove into the countryside to view the beautiful hills and buffalo country. Cookouts were quite enjoyable, but I never got used to the taste of the buffalo burger. We fished in the lake where historians state that Geronimo jumped on horseback and survived, but his horse did not.

In August 1962, I was promoted to first lieutenant. At that time, I was anxiously looking forward to February 1963 when I would complete my two-year military active-duty obligation. Therefore, I began to contact federal civil service authorities in an attempt to generate job interviews.

I soon learned my name was no longer on the federal register, nullifying my civil service eligibility. I had failed to annually notify civil service authorities of my continuing interest and not-available status due to active duty. In short, there I was, married with our second child, Sharon, and no job prospects. Consequently, I did not want to get out of the military with no job.

As a reserve officer on active duty, I requested and received a year extension. Approaching the end of my third year, Viola was pregnant with our third child, Janice. Surely, I didn't wish to chance getting out at that time. Long story short, my continuing requests for extensions on military active duty ended in retirement twenty-one years later (smile). I applied several times over the years but never received a Regular Army (RA) commission. As I approached my twenty-first year in 1981, I was finally offered a RA commission but instead chose to retire. As a note, beginning in 2006, all officers in the Army active component are commissioned RA.

In July of 1963, I was sent across the installation to attend the four-week Sergeant Officer Course covering the maintenance, operation, and employment of the Sergeant Missile, a nuclear weapons system. The Sergeant's mission was to attack and destroy major targets deep in enemy territory. Its seventy-five-mile range, its all-weather delivery capability, and its choice of nuclear, biological, or chemical warheads could wipe out enemy threats at a distance and of a magnitude far greater than was possible in World War II or even Korea. I graduated number four in a class of twenty-three with an average grade of 95.86 percent.

Chapter 8

Transfer to Germany

Second Unit Assignment

Following school, in September 1963, I was assigned to the Third Battalion, Eightieth Artillery, a Sergeant missile unit at Fort Sill, Oklahoma. Again, I was placed in the headquarters and headquarters battery and given duties associated with services rather than leadership. The unit had Sergeant missiles, and the entire battalion was slated to deploy to Germany. Initially, dependents were scheduled to join us at a later date. I was assigned the task of drafting a letter to the Commanding General, United States Army Europe, justifying why our dependents should accompany us simultaneously. That type of task of correspondence is normally assigned to the battalion adjutant, the administrative officer in an organization. In this case, my letter was dispatched to Europe, and the request to have our families accompany us to Germany was approved.

On September 14, 1964, I was promoted to the grade of captain. Soon thereafter, we departed Fort Sill, Oklahoma, and flew to Frankfurt, Germany. Viola and our three kids, Clifton, Sharon and Janice, all contracted chickenpox just before our departure. Once in Germany, we were housed in German hotels awaiting military housing. Needless to say, the German hotel owner didn't appreciate Blacks running around with white calamine lotion all over their faces.

I eventually had to go into the community and find housing for my family. Blacks were not the favorite people of German homeowners in the 1960s. Eventually, we located a house and lived there for several months.

Our home was surrounded by a no-see-through wall and gate. When viewing the home from the street, you could only see the second story of the house. This allowed my family a sense of anonymity.

Praise the Lord, I took German language classes in college. Perhaps six months later, we moved to a second-floor apartment in a military housing compound in Darmstadt, Germany.

The battalion headquarters was in the Ernst-Ludwig Kaserne in Darmstadt, Germany. We were about twenty miles south of Frankfurt. I was assigned as the Communications Platoon Leader and Survey Platoon Leader. Again, they weren't positions that normally led to career enhancement. I held those positions for several months, and my family was enjoying life in Germany. On the weekend, we drove or took train rides to various German cities and surrounding countries. It was a wonderful assignment for the family and a great experience for the kids to be exposed to a plethora of people and places.

Sharon, Janice and Clifton Jr., (circa 1966)

First Command Assignment

Being mindful that our battalion was a nuclear-capable unit with modern technical and sophisticated equipment, a separate unit was attached to us for command and operational control. The European Command decided to dissolve the battalion headquarters of the Third Target Acquisition Battalion, Twenty-sixth Artillery. That left two battery size units to operate independently, Battery A in Darmstadt and Battery B in Hanau, Germany.

Subsequently, the unit that I was a part of, the Third Battalion, Eightieth Artillery, was given the responsibility of serving as the battalion headquarters for the unit in Darmstadt. They were located in the same German Kaserne as our battalion. The battery's operational structure was not made a part of our battalion. The battery functions of personnel, intelligence, supply, and maintenance were kept separate and distinct from the similar battalion functions in our unit.

Battery A operated as a self-sustaining unit. In laymen's terms, our battalion was led by a lieutenant colonel, and a staff consisting of two majors, six or more captains, and numerous high-ranking enlisted personnel. The same functional responsibility was now thrust upon the captain commanding Battery A and his staff of lieutenants and enlisted personnel. Battery A still had to conduct personnel, intelligence, operations, and supply functions, in addition to duties once conducted by their defunct battalion headquarters.

Eventually, my battalion commander opined that the assigned battery commander for Battery A was not doing or could not do a good job. He thought it was the captain's fault that there were several operational problems and personnel problems involving personal and military vehicle accidents, troop involvement in German bar fights, etc.

My commander decided to relieve the battery commander and put me in command of the unit. Of course, I had no choice even if I wanted one. The battalion commander said I was the only captain in the battalion with a target acquisition background. I had been assigned to a target acquisition battalion at Fort Sill prior to our deployment to Germany.

Being in command of this abnormally organized unit was indeed a major challenge for several reasons. First, this was my first battery command assignment and secondly, the battery was attached to my old unit, the Third Battalion, Eightieth Artillery. There was absolutely nothing in common between the two organizations.

As a nuclear-capable unit, the Third Battalion, Eightieth Artillery was given high priority for highly skilled personnel and modern equipment. The unit was always deployed on smooth, hard-surfaced areas considered ideal for their highly technical equipment. The Army gave my new battery a lower priority for highly skilled personnel and modern equipment. We were deployed without regard to the adverse weather or surface conditions. Consequently, it was virtually impossible to maintain the standards in terms of personnel and equipment readiness demanded by the battalion commander and staff.

I took great pride in my unit personnel and, despite the challenges, learned a lot about people and performed my duties as best I could. The first thing I learned very early on was, as a leader, you must insulate your people from outside influencers. I once told my boss, the lieutenant colonel, that I would appreciate it very much if I were notified whenever he chose to enter my unit area. He had visited my motor pool area and chastised my motor sergeant about an infraction. He never did that again, and my people appreciated the fact that they worked for me, not him. He was my boss but not theirs.

My unit spent a lot of time at the Grafenwoehr Training Area in support of units undergoing training exercises. The diverse nature of the battery which included radar, survey, sound, flash, and a meteorological section made training, administration, and supply very difficult. The Radar Platoon employed radars in strategic locations on the make-believe battlefield to detect incoming missiles and projectiles. The Survey Platoon plotted location and directional information for the supported units. It was amazing to witness the survey personnel shooting angles on the North Star, the Big Dipper, etc., to determine exact locations. I learned more about the galaxy than I had ever learned while living in the dark countryside of Virginia. The Sound Platoon placed sound detectors all along the make-believe frontline to detect the location of enemy troops. The Flash Platoon applied a similar concept. The Meteorological Section actually sent up weather balloons to provide information to combat units and units in training exercises.

When deployed, my unit was spread out for many miles. The Grafenwoehr Training Area was 157 square miles. It was easy for various sections of my unit to be miles apart. To manage that operation was a challenge within itself. I designated a specific place for my key leaders to meet at the end of a training day. Often, it was a German restaurant within a gated compound. There, we could have a beer and discuss that day's activities and plan for the upcoming missions.

That reminds me of something very unique about being on maneuvers in Germany. Germany had Forestry Managers whose only job was to care for the forests. They normally lived in the area and monitored all activities associated with that forestry area. Germany had some of the most beautiful forestry areas in the world. When we went on military maneuvers, we had to be conscious of causing damage to any tree. For example, if our maneuvers caused damage to a three-foot tree, the Army had to reimburse the German government for the anticipated worth of that tree fully grown.

Today, I can barely believe I did it, but I sometimes traveled home to the family during training exercises. It was a three-hour trip by jeep from Grafenwoehr to Darmstadt. On Saturday night after the troops had bedded down, my German American driver Kovac and I made the trip to arrive at our homes around midnight. With instructions to pick me up by five in the morning. We arrived back to the training area in time to have breakfast at eight. As the commander, that was a dumb thing to do, and I'm sure my battalion commander would have relieved me had he known. To my knowledge and their credit, my people never told on me.

Commanding the uniquely organized unit was indeed a challenge, and I never felt I received the deserved credit for my performance of duty. In the military, your efficiency reports have a rater, endorser, and reviewer, in that order. My rater and endorser rendered an okay efficiency report, but it wasn't encouraging for an individual who wanted to be promoted.

Brigadier General (one-star) Fillmore K. Mearns was my reviewer at that time, and his input didn't make the report any better. I contacted him ten years later, after he had retired as a three-star lieutenant general to request his assistance in nullifying that report. Thankfully, he responded positively, and his letter of support is displayed later in this book.

Life in Germany

Our two-year stay in Germany was quite interesting.

For instance, it was routine for German homes to have bed linen hanging out of the window to be aired out during the day. It was normal for German natives to bathe once a week, and the goal was to use as little water as possible.

Shopping in the clothing stores in Frankfurt was an experience. We felt the quality of clothes was fantastic, well made with durable material. We took wonderful trips to nearby countries, often on the weekend. We even took a train trip to see the Berlin Wall. At stops along the way, communist soldiers checked the train, and it was quite a spectacle to watch them walk the train platform.

While visiting West Berlin, we got to visit Checkpoint Charlie along the Berlin wall. That was the location where President John F. Kennedy stated, "Ich bin ein Berliner!" on June 26, 1963.

To stand and look over the area between East and West Berlin was awesome. Of course, there was the cinderblock wall, concertina razor wire, and guard towers. Viola was allowed to take a tour on the East Berlin (communist) side, but I wasn't allowed to go because I had a top-secret clearance. The food in Berlin was fantastic. I love German food anyway.

The Autobahn in Germany was amazing. Mercedes, Audi, and Opel vehicles were popular. With no speed limit, it was normal to look in the rearview mirror and see blinking headlights of the cars coming up behind you. This was their way of letting you know they were approaching, so please stay out of the way. I have been passed going seventy miles per hour as though I were standing still.

Our family life continued to be quite interesting, even in Germany. Again, please remember that this was in the 1960s. Black officers were few and far between wherever we were stationed. When we attended social functions involving officers, we often found ourselves alone. We never felt welcome participating in the dynamics of activities with virtually all-White attendees. Consequently, Viola and I became close friends with several Black enlisted families who we socialized with as well as trusted with our kids. Intentionally, they were not in the same military organization. Of course, officers fraternizing with enlisted personnel was a no-no and was mentioned in one of my efficiency reports while stationed at Fort Sill.

Throughout my military career, we did have several White friends. A young enlisted family with the last name of Adams in Fort Sill, Oklahoma, befriended us when we arrived in 1961. Friends among commissioned officers' families included Walter Kinderman, William Copeland, and Carl Quickmire at Fort Knox, Kentucky, between 1974 and 1977. There seemed to have been pure harmony, love, and concern throughout those relationships. Periodic visitations and Christmas card exchanges continued for many, many years.

Leadership Guidance to Young Officers

Based on my first experience as a commander, this is an outline of the leadership guidance I provided to young military officers within my realm of influence. Much of this guidance is also applicable upon entry into a civilian job.

- Get Insurance
    - Automobile (be sure to do comparative shopping)
    - Term Life for the entire family which is convertible regardless of future health
- Organize and Maintain your Personal Records
    - Military (pay, temporary duty assignments, health and dental)
    - Non-military
- Get a Will
- Finance Actions
    - Temporary travel and duty assignments (find out your authorizations, use them, and be honest on your claims)
    - Savings (establish an allotment for long-term and emergency)
    - Checking account (have one accountant and NEVER let a check bounce)
    - Use credit unions and banks, never use finance companies (exorbitant interest rates). NOTE: Today I would add Payday and title loan shops to the list of never use
    - Live within a budget and below what you can afford
    - Don't co-sign any note unless you hold the payment book
    - Never rely on credit cards to survive
- Behavior
    - Maintain integrity at all times
    - Be loyal to everyone—superiors, peers, and subordinates
    - Avoid vulgarity and profanity
    - If you must drink alcohol, do it moderately and at appropriate times
    - Be honest and straightforward with everyone
    - Always find something kind to say to everyone you see each day
    - Praise your superiors to others, your subordinates to themselves and others, and yourself to no one
    - Be faithful to your loved ones
    - Don't use your rank. Use the respect gained by your rank and enhanced by your behavior

- Take care of your people; know their birthday and other special days, inquire about their spouse, children, mother, etc.
- Encourage your people to improve
- Be friendly with superiors and subordinates but don't become a friend. Maintain the true hierarchical relationship.
- Go to church
- Be sociable but keep family first
- Be level-headed but firm in your convictions
- Don't assume friendship or favoritism
- Military Jobs
  - Perform every job well. Know your job responsibility
  - Request an evaluation of your performance prior to receiving your official evaluation
  - Influence your assignments by requesting your preference before receiving orders
  - Use time wisely. Don't overdo overtime.
  - Plan your off-duty time as well as your duty time. Keep a list
  - Keep your boss informed on major matters to include shortcomings
  - Be open with your boss, and loyal after the decision
  - Be a good listener
  - Don't offer alibis or become argumentative
  - Periodically ask your boss to suggest ways to improve your effectiveness
  - Delegate authority properly and allow your subordinates to do their job. Normally, the more you comment on jobs well-done, the more you will have reasons to make that comment
  - Don't become known as an opportunist but capitalize on opportunities
  - **Tactfully** correct soldier appearance, behavior, etc.

Chapter 9

Germany Tour Cut Short

Fort Irwin, California, April 27, 1966

My family and I were enjoying our tour in Germany when I received orders to transfer to the Seventh Battalion, Ninth Artillery at Fort Irwin, California, cutting my Germany tour short by one year. The Army had activated the Seventh Battalion, Ninth Artillery for training and deployment to Vietnam in October 1966.

When we departed Germany and prior to reporting to Fort Irwin, California, we traveled to Virginia to visit our families in May 1966. One distinct incident I remember very vividly was my effort to uncover a window air conditioner at Viola's parents' home by standing on a lawn chair. Well, the chair flipped on me, and I ended up at the Fort Lee Military Hospital with a broken nose.

After our family visits, we headed for Fort Irwin, California, traveling on the infamous Route 66. Someone suggested that you should always have a pouch of water on the grill of the car. Supposedly this was to ward off the heat of the desert area and stop the car from overheating. Whether it was necessary or not, I didn't take a chance and placed a large pouch of water on the grill; my car didn't overheat.

After traveling three days on Route 66 West, we arrived in the city of Barstow, California. Turning northeast, we traveled thirty-five miles through the Mojave Desert and saw ONE homestead off in the desert before reaching Fort Irwin. Rumor has it that when that one homestead was no longer there, the front gate of Fort Irwin was moved closer to Barstow, allowing the government not to pay the Fort Irwin soldiers separation pay (smile).

In 1966, there was very little activity at Fort Irwin, but it was an interesting place. It was used for National Guard and Reserve training, plus it served as the Armored Combat Training Area during the Korean War. In later years, Fort Irwin was dedicated as the Army National Training Center, and the post bubbled with activity. With the buildup of the Vietnam War, the Army activated the Seventh Battalion, Ninth Artillery, a towed 105-mm howitzer unit, for the sole purpose of being ramped up for deployment to Vietnam.

Believe me, we had plenty of desert area to conduct training. Except for sporadic wooded areas, there were miles and miles of plain desert. The firing range of the 105-mm howitzer is up to eight miles, with the high explosive projectile having a killing radius of more than fifty meters. Perhaps we were the first artillery unit to undergo training at Fort Irwin because it appeared we had the entire area to ourselves.

After departing Germany as a unit commander, I had thought that my new assignment was going to be a similar career-enhancing one. I didn't get a command position as I had hoped. I was again given the position of communications officer, a non-career enhancing position.

To properly equip the battalion for training and combat, we were issued state-of-the-art vehicles and other equipment. The major exception was our radios and communications equipment. There was a five-month delay to receive the new communications equipment, and we had to commence training. The new radios were to arrive later. There were older vehicular radios available on the base that were used by the National Guard and Reserve units who trained there. They were not designed to be mounted on the new generation of military vehicles issued to us.

Rather than drill holes into our new vehicles for them to be unused later, I designed a fabricated mount that allowed the old radios to be mounted without a single hole in our new vehicles. Upon receipt, our new radios, which were designed for our vehicles, were mounted without a hitch.

Introduction to Death Valley

While Fort Irwin was thirty-five miles northeast of Barstow, traveling ten additional miles in the same direction took me through a mountain range into Death Valley. There is flat terrain for miles and miles. Traveling farther in the same direction from the mountain range, I was completely lost with no reference of direction to return to the spot from whence I came. Unless you've been there, it's difficult to imagine the awesomeness of Death Valley.

On Sunday, July 16, 1966, Second Lieutenant Arthur Rowland Jr., and Specialist Fourth Class Jeffrey L. Cullimore decided they were going to venture into the Mohave Desert to hunt for unusual rocks.

They had not returned by Monday morning, so their unit commander put out a request for help to find them. My battalion commander ordered the entire unit to join the search in the Mohave Desert. By nightfall, we had reached the mountain range near the entrance into the Death Valley area, and there was no sign of the missing men. We set up a command center to continue the search the next day. While it's as hot as 120 degrees during the day, the desert gets cold at night. The next day (Tuesday), we were sent out in two-vehicle pairs, instructed to never lose sight of each other. Once we maneuvered through the mountain pass onto the Death Valley area, we could see for miles.

There were small mounds, clusters of desert foliage, but no living animal or person in our sight, even though Death Valley is notorious for reptiles and other creatures. Occasionally, we came upon areas where water was barely under the surface and made the ground soft; fortunately, our vehicle didn't get stuck. Plus, we found areas that had evidence of prospector activities long ago—a tin cup, a glass bottle, etc. We searched for two days and found no sign of the missing men. Several other units continued the search, and Second Lieutenant Rowland's body was finally found on Saturday night, four miles from his jeep, which was out of fuel. To my knowledge, Specialist Fourth Class Cullimore was never found. It's thought that his helmet liner was found several miles from the jeep.

As fate would have it, a young Army captain from Los Angeles was sent to escort the lieutenant's body home. That captain was Paul Sample, one of my high school classmates. I didn't learn he was there until our high school reunion in 2019, when Paul and I saw each other for the first time in nearly sixty years. We talked about the event at Fort Irwin, and I learned he had married the widow of the deceased lieutenant. Not only that, his wife had resided on the Eastern Shore while he was in Vietnam at the same time Viola was on the Eastern Shore while I was in Vietnam. Viola and his wife had become friends in our absence. Of course, when Viola told me she was friends with Paul Sample's wife, we didn't make the Fort Irwin connection.

Relocation of Family to Virginia

After three months of training at Fort Irwin, the unit was ordered to deploy to Vietnam in October 1966. Consequently, I moved my family to the Eastern Shore of Virginia for them to reside with my parents while I was in Vietnam. At this time, we had three kids—Clifton Jr., Sharon, and Janice. Ronald and Donald were born two months later in December. I will talk later about receiving notification of their birth and my reaction.

Overnight, the number of occupants in my parents' home had grown from three (my parents and my brother Lafayette) to seven with Viola and three kids. And it would grow to nine occupants in a matter of two more months. Plus, five of those occupants were five years old or younger. My parents were amazing to accept my family into their modest home.

During my youth, there was always a pail available in the house at night that served as bathroom accommodations. During the day, year-round, no matter how hot or cold the weather was, the family was required to use the outhouse. I was always afraid a snake or spider would bite my butt as I sat over the hole. Of course, real toilet tissue was never available, only pages from a Sears Roebuck or Montgomery Ward's catalog served as toilet tissue.

Viola and the kids weren't used to outhouses. Consequently, Viola and I agreed to have an indoor bathroom installed with a tub, commode, and shower. Living rent-free allowed us to bear the expense. My parents enjoyed having indoor bathroom accommodations.

Chapter 10

First Deployment to Vietnam

Trip on Troop Ship and Arrival in Vietnam

In October 1966, our entire unit with all its equipment was put on the USNS Barrett troop ship in San Diego, California, and we spent twenty-six days on the water enroute to Vietnam. The most revolutionary feature on the ship was complete air-conditioning.

My research indicated the ship was retired in 1973 and was awaiting disposal in the James River Reserve Fleet in Newport News, Virginia. I also learned that a scrapping contract was awarded to Bay Bridge Enterprises, in Chesapeake, Virginia, on June 13, 2007, for $851,194. Since I live a football field distance from the Newport News border, I rushed to check it out in October 2020. It was no longer there. Apparently, the scrapping was completed.

There were probably well over 1,500 Army, Navy, and Marine Corps troops onboard, many of whom had never been on a ship. Many troops had never been on even a rowboat. Seasickness was a big problem. One individual getting seasick made everybody around them sick. I soon found out why empty fifty-five-gallon drums were placed around the main deck.

The challenge was to keep the troops occupied. There were numerous life jacket drills, plus, special service personnel organized bands, card games, and other activities. Of course, gambling was forbidden, but how would you punish the guilty? Send them to Vietnam?

As you may have guessed, I was assigned as the troop commander for the voyage, which was a glorified title for the chief housekeeper. Officers and senior enlisted personnel were assigned to staterooms while the troops were below deck in troop compartments. My major responsibility was to ensure the maintenance of clean and safe troop living areas. This responsibility applied to all on board, including the Navy and Marine Corps personnel. I was struck by the fact that whenever I inspected the Army areas, I was normally escorted by a commissioned officer. However, my escort in the Marine Corps areas was a Sergeant, and their areas were always up to par.

Twenty-six days on the vast ocean brought about a lot of seasickness. I ensured the living areas and gangways were properly cleaned and sanitized. That responsibility reflected the typical assignment for a Black officer in the 1960s. Perhaps, I'm being too critical.

Since I was the battalion communications officer, I also taught classes during the voyage on various modes of communications to include cryptographic security. Physical training and basic military skill training such as map reading took place daily on the ship's deck.

After twenty-three long days on the water, we made one overnight stop in Okinawa for the ship to be refueled and resupplied. We arrived near sunset and were allowed to debark that evening. There wasn't much to do, for we certainly weren't thinking of buying souvenirs enroute to combat. Setting sail the next morning, we arrived in Vietnam three days later. The Marines were dropped off in Da Nang, and we debarked in the Vietnamese city of Vung Tau.

We were flown to Phu Loi, north of Saigon on October 26, 1966. The Phu Loi Base Camp (also known as Darkhorse Base or Phu Loi Field) was occupied by the Eleventh Air Cavalry Regiment. It was obvious that much vehicular activity had taken place in the camp because it was basically a mud hole.

For about two weeks, we lived in pup tents and quickly learned how it felt to be in wet clothes all day. It rained all the time, and it was hot and muggy. Everyone was required to take salt pills daily. We were issued jungle boots, jungle fatigues, armored vests, and steel helmets. Knowing your life may be saved by adorning those items, it didn't take long to get comfortable having the heavy helmet on your head and hot and heavy vest on your person every waking hour.

Bear Cat, an old abandon ranger camp, was selected to be the permanent home base for our battalion under the control of the Fifty-fourth Artillery Group of the II Field Force. It was an U.S. Army Special Forces base near the city of Bien Hòa in Dong Nai Province in southern Vietnam. The base was about one-mile square surrounded by a high berm of dirt. There were two entrances manned by the First Special Forces.

Our Headquarters (HQ) Battery and the B Battery relocated to the Bear Cat base camp on November 10, 1966. The Service Battery arrived on November 13, 1966, and the battalion was considered completely operational on November 14, 1966. On November 21, 1966, I was relieved of my communications officer duties and designated the HQ battery commander with the responsibility to get the battalion settled.

The A Battery remained at Phu Loi until November 24, 1966 and participated in the first major combat operation of the battalion. While there, the battery fired in support of elements of the Second Battalion, Second Infantry Division when they were attacked by an enemy force estimated to be 300 to 400 Viet Cong. This action resulted in forty-three Viet Cong dead by body count. On November 24, the A Battery moved to Bear Cat to join the battalion. On November 14, 1966, C Battery was moved to Xuan Loc and remained there until January 13, 1967, when the unit joined the battalion at Bear Cat.

The First Special Forces had established a base at Bear Cat, and we were joined in January 1967 by the Ninth Infantry Division, a welcomed addition for base security.

Command of Headquarters and Headquarters Battery, Seventh Battalion, Ninth Artillery

From November 21, 1966, until April 11, 1967, I was the commanding officer of the Headquarters and Headquarters Battery (HHB) of the battalion. My responsibilities were centered around housekeeping—housing, messing, health, and welfare. As the HHB commander, I was responsible for the safety and welfare of 20 officers, 3 warrant officers, and 120 enlisted personnel. In total, the battalion consisted of 35 officers, 3 warrant officers, and 495 enlisted personnel. Because we had arrived in Vietnam as a unit, there was an exchange of personnel with other units who had arrived earlier or later. This was to ensure everyone in our unit didn't have the same date of departure a year later.

The WABTOC (When Authorized by The Overseas Commander) materials for the battalion arrived at the Saigon port on November 23, 1966. Between November 25 and 28, twenty-four five-ton truckloads and forty-six two-and-a-half-ton truckloads of materials were moved from the Saigon docks to our base camp. All materials were hauled by the battalion's organic equipment.

Bear Cat had a few buildings occupying a small portion of the camp belonging to the First Special Forces. Apparently anticipating the moving in of additional American units, the camp had been sprayed with Agent Orange. We were directed to the southern end of the camp where it was very difficult to find hard dry areas to set up tents or park our equipment. The major portion of the camp was obviously held for the anticipated move in of the Ninth Infantry Division.

Our area of the base had to be fortified and made livable. Maneuvering in the muddy area and sleeping in tents was not fun. Living under the constant enemy probing of our perimeter and threat to myself and my personnel was quite a mental strain. Eventually, we managed to make our area more livable. Using local Vietnamese craftsmen, we constructed buildings. Beginning with virtually nothing, we procured the lumber and Vietnamese carpenters to construct four enlisted billets, two officer quarters, a battalion aid station, a dining hall, and a battalion headquarters building. All necessary facilities, offices, and billets were constructed within four months of moving into the area.

Each structure had raised wooden floors to counter the muddy conditions. The paths between structures were either wooden sidewalks or a hard, reddish, clayey, topsoil material called laterite. Eventually, we moved out of the pup tents. We even constructed showers from corrugated steel sheets and used emergency heaters to heat the water.

A new building being constructed (You can see temporary facilities in the background), December 1966

At that time, I was a captain, and one of my main go-to enlisted soldiers was Staff Sergeant Julius Coats. SSG Coats was in my supply section, and when I needed building supplies, I simply provided SSG Coats with the required paperwork and some bargaining items. He left Bear Cat with a convoy of empty trucks, went to the Long Bien supply area near Saigon, and returned in the evening with five or more loads of lumber; everything we needed to construct buildings.

There were always Vietnamese carpenters available to earn a good salary to do the work. They were extremely talented with their hands and constructed outstanding facilities. Often, SSG Coats also brought back steaks and other delicious delicacies. I'm pleased to report that SSG Coats survived his Vietnam tour and later became a commissioned officer, reaching the rank of full bird colonel by the time of his retirement. He and his beautiful wife Patsy currently reside less than ten minutes from where I live. We have had a long, enduring friendship over the years.

Having been on maneuvers in Germany and elsewhere, I was used to sleeping in pup tents and eating c-rations. This was different. We also had to be mindful of being in enemy territory at all times. You always had to have a pistol on your hip or a rifle in your hand. Every time you heard an unusual noise, you were mindful it could be the enemy.

The Vietnam populace were in severe poverty by our standards, living in shacks with tin roofs, dirt or often wood floors, and no electricity or bathrooms. Vietnamese people appeared to be generally short and thin, and extremely friendly. We attempted to have a good relationship with the villagers by assisting wherever possible, such as donating food to the Queen of Peace Orphanage in Bien Hoa and building a roof for the village school in Hauoc Nguyen. Often our medical personnel visited nearby villages to offer medical support. Whenever we left the camp, the Vietnamese men were often seen with their oxen working in the knee-deep water of the rice paddles. The unsettling dilemma was that you never really knew who the enemy was. The same Vietnamese barber who was allowed in the area to cut your hair today may be a Viet Cong guerrilla by night.

During the monsoon season, we were always soaking wet. Viola had given me a small New Testament Bible which I carried in the top left pocket of my uniform. It stayed wet. Whenever I prayed or needed God's encouragement, I simply reached up and held my hand over my pocket. This action gave me peace. I totally depended on God. After a couple of weeks in Vietnam, I didn't worry about my survival, for I felt God was in control, and there was absolutely nothing I could do about what happened. I had to completely depend on Him.

In December of 1966, I received a phone call from the American Red Cross. "Captain Collins, you are hereby notified your wife and newly born boys are doing fine."

"Boys, what do you mean boys?"

"Your wife has given birth to twin boys."

Viola and I had no idea she was pregnant with twins.

To my knowledge, ultrasound was not being utilized for pregnancies at that time. Viola later told me when the first boy was delivered, the doctor said, "Hold on. There's another one."

Well, I was so excited I told my driver to get a volunteer to man the jeep-mounted machine gun, and we went to Tan Son Nhat Air Force Base to send flowers. The base was twenty-seven miles away and the largest American installation in the area. Even though the route had not been declared secure, I didn't want to miss this opportunity to convey my elation to my sweetheart. We made the trip and returned to camp safely.

Viola sent my first picture of the twins (Ronald and Donald), along with Clifton Jr, Sharon, and Janice, plus my brother Lafayette who was a great helper for Viola. April 1967

During the five months I commanded the HHB, we developed our area into one of the finest base camps, considering the circumstances. I quickly learned, under combat conditions, the entire unit became like a family. We depended on each other to survive. Of course, everyone had their personalities, prejudices, biases, and hatreds, but it didn't last long after arrival in-country.

At that time, I was living in a two-person hooch with my White roommate Doctor H. Bland Hudgins, the battalion physician, from Mathews County, Virginia. He was an extremely nice person, and we got along great. Since we arrived in Vietnam at the same time, we returned to the States also at about the same time. I was assigned to Fort Monroe and kept thinking I was going to look him up and visit. I learned he was a practicing *civilian* doctor living less than fifty miles from my home.

As I often say, don't procrastinate or you'll have regrets later. During a medical appointment, I met a couple who knew Dr. Hudgins, and they informed me he died in 2007 at the young age of sixty-eight. Oh, how I wish I had looked him up earlier.

Once the billets, mess hall, and other comfort structures had been completed, daily life wasn't that bad. There was a place to shower, sit and eat comfortably, sleep comfortably, read books, etc. We only had to worry about our perimeter being breached and receiving incoming rockets and mortar rounds. That didn't happen in the five months I was commanding the unit. We often heard combat activity a distance from our base but never on our position.

One fateful day, my commander called me to his office and stated that C Battery was experiencing some personnel problems, and I was to assume command of that unit. Mind you, I was being sent from a comfortable living situation to a truer combat situation. Being in the military, you merely salute and carry on. The next morning, I was on a helicopter heading for a spot in the jungle.

After a brief discussion with the departing commander, who I knew well, I was in command of C Battery, Seventh Battalion, Ninth Artillery.

Command of C Battery, Seventh Battalion, Ninth Artillery

I was reassigned as the commander of C Battery from April 12 through September 1, 1967. It was a drastic change from commanding a hospitality operation to commanding an active combat unit in the middle of the jungle, but I loved the change of atmosphere and responsibility. Although I had been the Headquarters and Headquarters Battery commander, I was always in the daily presence of several officers who outranked me. When I took over C Battery, I was the senior officer in the area. No one in the area outranked me. I had full responsibility for five other officers and 111 enlisted personnel.

Plus, often I had operational control and responsibility for other attached units. It was my job to lead, direct, feed, and protect everyone while carrying out C Battery's mission of supporting all fighting units within a seven to eight-mile radius of our position. The fighting units included American, South Vietnamese, Korean, Australian, and other friendly units throughout the Third Corps area.

First Sergeant Langster Being Shaved, Loc Ninh, Republic of Vietnam, April 1967

First Sergeant Langster (1SG) was the senior noncommissioned officer (NCO) in my unit. He considered Lawton, Oklahoma, to be his home. He was one of the most loyal people I ever had the pleasure of working with. In the photo, note the rank insignia on his shirt sleeve, three stripes up, three stripes down, with a diamond in the middle (rank of E-8). He supervised and received the respect of the entire unit. His primary responsibility was the supervision of the administrative, disciplinary, morale, nutriment, and medical care of the unit. In other words, he answered only to me and basically ran the unit. I was there to provide guidance, make decisions, and take responsibility for the good and not so good.

My chief of fire was Sergeant First Class (SFC) Taggart (rank of E-7), a red-headed soldier from Alabama. He was responsible for the personnel and equipment associated with the six 105mm howitzer crews. A super NCO, his leadership in providing artillery support to friendly troops was unparalleled.

SFC Taggart, me & Specialist E-4 Fidel, Loc Ninh, Republic of Vietnam, April 1967

Both 1SG Langster and SFC Taggart were perhaps forty years old with twenty years or more years of Army experience. I credit those two gentlemen for ushering our unit through a year of combat duty with no major personnel or combat issues. I owe them a heap of gratitude. It's amazing what's possible when a group is working together for a common cause.

My other close associate was my driver, Specialist E-4 (SPC) Fidel. He was from Mississippi. Considering the circumstances, that young man kept my jeep in top operating condition and immaculate. He even fabricated seat covers

SPC Fidel, Loc Ninh, Republic of Vietnam, April 1967

and headrests using parachute cloth and ammo containers. Also, sandbags covered the floor of the jeep to hopefully absorb the impact of a road mine.

SPC Fidel never questioned my decisions and willingly served as my driver regardless of the looming danger. Most important, he was dependable and calm during times of enemy activity. When in combat, cool heads must prevail if you wish to stay alive. For instance, by the book, when an artillery battery convoys from one position to another, the convoy is led by the firing battery lieutenant. Well, I often led the convoys, thinking I was more sensitive to indicators of imminent ambushes and road mines. Additionally, he often offered to dig my foxhole. Unless I had something more pressing, I typically dug my own foxhole and prepared my sleeping area. I will never forget his loyalty.

For my grandchildren and others who have never been in the military, I will attempt to paint a clearer picture of the typical daily activities of my 105mm howitzer artillery unit while in Vietnam. There were six howitzers, each weighing 5,000 pounds and being towed by a two-and-a-half-ton truck. Each howitzer had an eight-man crew who ate and slept near the howitzer twenty-four hours a day, seven days a week.

Each member had a specific function to perform in order to load, aim, and fire as many as 200 thirty-pound projectiles from the weapon daily. Upon arrival in an area, the howitzers were maneuvered into a star-like formation. This ensured we had the capability of firing at least one gun in any direction needed within thirty seconds of the request for support from a friendly unit in trouble. By the time the fire of that one gun was adjusted on the target, the other five guns had been maneuvered into position and ready to fire for maximum effect onto the enemy target.

The 105mm howitzer can propel a thirty-six-inch-long projectile weighing thirty-two pounds seven miles and strike within fifty meters of the target. Imagine the six projectiles exploding around you every ten seconds. The ammunition available included high explosive, smoke, illumination, white phosphorous, and the beehive anti-personnel projectile. On a normal day, we fired the howitzers fifteen times, averaging more than a hundred rounds.

Previous wars had the "frontline" and "rear area" distinctly delineated on the battle maps, so there was a feeling of safety while in the rear. This was not the case in Vietnam. There was no frontline or rear area. There was a constant twenty-four-hour awareness of a potential combat situation 360 degrees around our position. So, we had to be prepared to fire in any direction.

This level of engagement was required to fulfill fifteen to thirty daily requests for help from friendly troops engaged in combat with the enemy. Since there was no combat frontline, each infantry or fighting unit was assigned a specific area to search for and destroy the enemy. My unit was assigned to provide artillery support for that fighting unit, and in turn, they were responsible for leaving a contingency of their personnel behind to protect us.

Once the howitzers were in position, the chief of fire set out alignment poles to synch the guns' location with the geographical map of the area. In the meantime, the crews immediately began to fortify their area by filling sandbags. The outside perimeter of each gun position was sandbagged, followed by interior sandbagged areas. Included were recessed sleeping areas for the eight-man crew for each howitzer. All of this had to be done by nightfall.

The goal was to be fortified before sundown. Of course, the enemy struck at any time, but we certainly had a better chance of defending ourselves if we were fortified. We definitely didn't want darkness to come before we were ready.

When my unit was located at airfields or other hardtop areas, we put up individual pup tents and surrounded them with sandbag barriers. Unless we had a direct hit, we could withstand a mortar or rocket attack.

When the fighting unit sent a patrol (group) out in search of the enemy, I sent one of my lieutenants with the patrol. My lieutenant's responsibility as forward observer was to communicate with my control center if there was a need for artillery support. He had to always know exactly where he was on the map. When the patrol found the enemy or the enemy found them, my forward observer requested we fire one howitzer at a specific spot on the map.

Based on where we were located and where the projectile landed, he instructed us to adjust the location of the explosion. For example, "left 300 and add 200," meant change our direction (aim) so the projectile would land 300 meters to the left and 200 meters beyond where the first projectile landed. We fired the one howitzer again, and he might say, "Add one hundred and fire for effect." In layman's terms, move the explosion one hundred meters beyond the last one and fire all six howitzers until I tell you to stop. By this time, the other five howitzers have been maneuvered into position pointing in the same direction as the adjusting howitzer, and all six howitzers were ready to fire at the same time. The next six projectiles would hit the desired location onto the enemy. The firing continued until our forward observer was satisfied the enemy had been eliminated. When we fired the six howitzers, the explosives covered an area nearly the size of sixteen football fields arranged four by four. There was no room for error that may chance hitting the friendly troops.

We never knew how long we'd be in a certain location. This was particularly true for my unit because we weren't assigned to a specific division. Therefore, we went wherever there was a need for support. Had we belonged to a specific division, such as the First or Twenty-fifth Infantry Division, we would have been operating in a specific area.

Captain Clifton Collins Sr. at One of Six Typical Gun Positions, Loc Ninh, Republic of Vietnam, April 1967

Gun crews slept within the sandbagged circular bunker surrounding their howitzer. There were recessed areas to accommodate the crew personnel as well as sufficient ammunition to support most missions. Troops who were not members of the gun crews had to dig personal foxholes and sleeping areas, reinforced with sandbags, and covered by pup tents. The foxholes had to be long and deep enough for your reclining body on an army cot to be below surface level. On top of the foxhole were several rows of metal poles covered with sandbags. An opening on one end large enough for your body to get through was left. Then, a pup tent was placed over the sandbagged space to keep the constant rainwater out. A drainage ditch had to be dug around the space to also keep the rainwater out.

The typical sleeping accommodations: personal items stored on top/sleep area below sandbags; Loc Ninh, Republic of Vietnam, April 1967

The space on top of the sandbags and beneath the tent was for storing personal items. In the picture, the sleeping area is the dark space below the sandbags. When ready to rest, we slid under the sandbagged cover like a snake. Often, a snake may have joined us (smile). Fortunately, I never personally had a snake companion to my knowledge. Being so afraid of snakes, I would have certainly vacated the area in a hurry.

No matter how often or how many sandbags were filled, we never wanted to be left vulnerable to the enemy. Plus, if my unit was not properly fortified, a visiting dignitary in my chain of command would have relieved me on the spot. Lieutenant General William E. DePuy was notorious for doing that. He always traveled with a captain as his aide. If he determined a commander had not properly secured his unit, he would simply relieve that commander and leave his aide in charge until a new commander was assigned.

Captain Clifton Collins Sr. by his sleeping area, Loc Ninh, Republic of Vietnam, April 1967

Captain Clifton Collins Sr. with his driver SPC Fidel next to him, and two members of an 105mm Howitzer Crew, Loc Ninh, Republic of Vietnam, April 1967.

The two-and-a-half-ton truck associated with each howitzer was parked nearby and loaded with various projectiles, small arms ammunition, sandbags, tents, and personal items. Each vehicle was loaded identically. In the heat of battle, every soldier knew where to find what was needed, even if it wasn't the truck associated with his gun crew. In other words, if illumination projectiles were needed, any crew member knew exactly where to find the projectile even in the dark. It's amazing what can be accomplished when people work together.

In the meantime, while we were busy fortifying our gun positions, the infantry unit assigned to protect us was fortifying their positions on the perimeter. Foxholes were dug, claymore mines and tripwires were placed out front, and fields of fire were coordinated so every path of approach by the enemy was covered. While all of these activities were going on, we were often interrupted by requests for fire support from a friendly unit in a battle with the enemy. The battle would often go on for hours.

Because artillery units didn't have the weaponry nor personnel to protect themselves, there was always an infantry unit (American, Vietnamese, or Korean) assigned to provide us perimeter protection. My ability to sleep peacefully night or day depended on my confidence in the perceived ability of the surrounding unit to protect us.

On one occasion when a Vietnamese unit arrived, they had their families with them, which was not uncommon. Well, while they should have been setting up our defense several yards out around our position, a Vietnamese soldier had actually used a tent pole on my tent for one end of his hammock. That was quickly corrected (smile).

Our connection with the units being supported was primarily through the Fire Support Officers (FSO) or Forward Observers (FO). FSOs and/or FOs were attached to the combat units to ensure the receipt of air and/or artillery support as needed. The FSO/FO attached to units we were supporting communicated their requests to my operations section. The operations section, using a flat board with a protractor and ruler on a map, determined the angle and distance and passed the correct commands to the guns. Our mission was to have those projectiles on the way in less than a minute.

Overhead visibility was a concern. Rain was almost a daily phenomenon in Vietnam. Often there was thick morning fog which degraded the capability of receiving support from the air. In other words, the jet and helicopter pilots didn't have clear visibility to see their targets if we came under attack. Every morning we prayed for clear skies. Air force jet fighters and Army gunships saved many friendly troops' lives in Vietnam. It was my understanding that visibility was no problem for the B-52 bombers. The eight-engine Stratofortress could fly completely out of sight, but when they dropped the bombs, we felt the earth shake for miles.

As an artillery unit, we didn't experience the type of combat activity as an infantry, armor, or Marine unit. We had to worry about our convoy being hit while relocating from one position to another or being hit while in position. We were constantly relocating from place-to-place under the threat of ambushes, attacks, and incoming rockets and mortars.

Most of the American strategy was based on "search and destroy" which meant infantry and mechanized units deliberately went into the jungle to search and destroy the enemy. I can't imagine having to wade waist-deep through swampy areas not knowing when I might encounter a booby-trap, a land mine, or the enemy himself.

Even when units were being attacked, infantry personnel were taken to the fight by helicopters. Often the drop zones were hot, meaning the enemy was firing on the drop-off area. Unfortunately, soldiers of color appeared to have been overrepresented in units that were in constant direct conflict with the enemy.

Particularly at night, we heard rifle fire, bombing, and other combat noises. On one occasion in An Loc, we were the target. After withstanding incoming rockets and mortars in our vicinity, but not directly on our position, I couldn't remember what had taken place. Later, I was informed that while under attack, I ran from bunker to bunker ensuring the safety of my personnel. I was still in my underclothes. That wasn't too cool. A leader must stay calm (smile).

We never knew when we might be called upon to relocate two or more of our howitzers to support a friendly unit who found themselves beyond the range of our location. The selected gun crews with an infantry unit escort would relocate and position to ensure mutual support from our base position. If the distance and circumstances dictated, we requested the howitzers with crews be airlifted utilizing crane helicopters. During lulls in activity, we trained on the method of rigging the howitzers and equipment to be airlifted.

I vividly recall our move to the An Loc Air Field and being attached to the First Infantry Division. Our primary mission was direct support to Task Force Dixie and base camp defense of Quan Loi. Later, we moved up the road about three miles to Loc Ninh where I met an orphan boy who rode in my jeep. He had been living in our camp for about three months when I rotated back to the United States. He was ten years old, and I often wonder what happened to him. Because there was no such thing as a combat frontline during the Vietnam War, we had to be mindful the enemy could be anywhere. Fortunately, I deemed him not to be an enemy. He assisted us on several occasions when dealing with the townspeople.

Letter Writing Time, April 1967

The resupply helicopter visited us at least once a week, bringing us food and supplies but, most importantly, mail. I attempted to write home every day. It was therapeutic to me. Viola kept my letters; however, they were lost during our many later relocations in the States. They certainly would have been useful for this project.

When we had a break in combat activity, we conducted cannoneer drills to increase speed and improve the accuracy of our artillery fire. My fire direction personnel conducted team drills to increase proficiency in fire direction procedures.

When I took command in April 1967, the C Battery was attached to the First Infantry Division and located at An Loc and later moved to Loc Ninh. On six occasions, portions (normally two howitzers) of the battery were displaced to support search and destroy operations conducted by maneuver battalions. On May 5, 1967, we displaced from Loc Ninh to Vuan Loi and later to Quan Loi to provide base camp defense again for the First Infantry Division. On July 6, my unit was released from attachment to the First Infantry Division and returned to our battalion base camp at Bear Cat. The C Battery had been providing daily combat support for nearly four months without a break. Everyone was happy to get a hot shower and sit at a table to eat.

While we were commended for providing artillery support for several combat events, we were also thankful to not have any casualties, and our medical aid men had benevolently medically treated many Vietnamese civilians and children.

On July 26, we were attached to the Ninth Infantry Division with mission of direct support to the Fifty-second Army of the Republic of Vietnam (ARVN) Battalion operating south of our home base near the Rung Sat Special Zone, a notorious area for the Viet Cong forces to concentrate. I positioned my unit on the grounds of the abandoned Bin Son French Rubber Plantation for the five-day mission. French rubber plantations were very common and desirable with large open clear areas for my gun emplacements.

When we arrived at the plantation, I was greeted by Captain Guthrie Ashton, a classmate from Virginia State College (now University). He was a staff officer in the Second Battalion, Thirty-ninth Infantry Regiment, also with the mission to provide support to the ARVN battalion. The fact that my classmate and I were

Vietnamese Kids enjoying our refreshments provided by our unit, Vuan Loi Vietnam, July 1967

jointly providing combat assistance to an ARVN fighting unit was absolutely amazing.

At this time in my life, I was in a combat situation and often thinking about my wife and five kids back home. So, when I saw Vietnamese kids, I felt great empathy for them.

Occasionally, I was required to personally return to base camp and managed to catch a hop on Air America planes to Tan Son Nhat Airport near Saigon. Air America was an airline covertly operated by the Central Intelligence Agency (CIA). They were crude propeller planes with walk-up ramps in the rear and a few web-type seats on each side. Already on the plane would be several Vietnamese families with bags of rice, live chickens and pigs. Those were interesting flights.

While commanding C Battery, I witnessed the second battle of Bau Bang which took place March 19-20, 1967, from a distance of about three miles. North Vietnamese troops drove and followed behind a herd of water buffalos towards B Battery's position. Between our rounds of illumination coupled with illumination from the air force, the battle area could be seen for miles. The following morning, we were told the North Vietnamese soldiers were probably doped up on betel nut or some other drug, because they never ceased to charge the American position, in wave after wave. My unit fired hundreds of rounds of supportive artillery during that all-night battle. With the illumination, soldiers stated they could very easily see the charging North Vietnamese, and they continued to repel them with the anti-personnel projectiles.

An internet search reports there were only 3 friendly deaths and 63 wounded compared to 227 enemies dead and 3 captured. The only time the anti-personnel projectiles could be used in Vietnam was against swarming attacks of Viet Cong or North Vietnamese soldiers threatening to overrun your unit's position. The anti-personnel projectiles are loaded with thousands of flechettes and were considered inhumane. The flechettes often pinned the enemy's arms to his body. Praise the Lord, my unit never had to employ anti-personnel ammunition.

Many times, we were directed to simply fire the six howitzers all night to harass the enemy. If we were near mountains, we fired into the mountains to improve our chances that nobody was there trying to set up mortars to hit us. I often wondered how many innocent women and children we may have wounded or killed.

I lost three dear friends in the Vietnam War. Major Willie Brickhouse was a helicopter pilot from my hometown who was shot down. First Lieutenant Ruppert L. Sargent was a college classmate who jumped on two grenades thrown by the enemy during a battle on March 15, 1967, to save his troops and was fatally wounded. He was the first Black officer to ever receive the Medal of Honor.

On October 31, 1967, Captain Riley L. Pitts was leading his unit in a battle and hurled a grenade at the enemy, but it bounced back into his area. In his effort to save his troops, he jumped on it but it didn't detonate. He got up and continued to rally his troops and eventually was fatally wounded. He also received the Medal of Honor. Captain Pitts and I had served together at Fort Sill, Oklahoma, as lieutenants.

On a more pleasant note, I will never forget an event that took place one day in the middle of the jungle. A Hiller OH-23 Raven Helicopter circled my unit's position and began to descend, blowing our materials everywhere. That type of helicopter normally denoted the arrival of a bigwig. Once landed, the pilot was the only passenger. I was indeed surprised when I recognized the pilot as William "Baby" Bailey, my Eastern Shore homeboy, Kappa line brother, and dear friend. He had contacted my battalion headquarters and learned of my unit's location.

Captain Clifton Collins Sr. and Homeboy Captain William Bailey,
March 1967

The picture of Bailey and me has been damaged over the years, but this is us standing in front of his helicopter with the howitzer positions on the left and right of us in the background. Later, I learned he had already been awarded a Purple Heart after receiving a bullet through the shoulder while attempting to extract troops from a gunfight in the Vietnam countryside. For him to fly solo over the jungles of Vietnam only to see me will never be forgotten.

I needed that boost. I was a little uptight with concern for our security. That visit, more than fifty-five years ago, will forever remain in my memory, and I thank Brother Bailey every time I'm in his presence.

I don't remember the racial breakdown of my soldiers, but I must say we didn't experience the racial problems seen back home in America. There may have been incidents kept away from me as the "old man." My soldiers seem to have gotten along very well. and I never suffered insubordination throughout my command time.

While Blacks accounted for a high percentage of the total troops in Vietnam, only a small number were officers. Black commanders were not seen very often. My soldiers never questioned my leadership demands to "dig in," "pack up and let's get ready to move," "prepare to be airlifted to" wherever, or "maintain blackout." Participating in military combat tends to promote harmony among the personnel. In my unit in Vietnam, there never seemed to have been a Black/White issue. Race wasn't a subject of discussion. There was a common bond where everyone depended on each other for safety and survival.

The Twenty-fifth Infantry Division was located in Cu Chi, Vietnam, and commanded by then Major General Fillmore K. Mearns. On one occasion, I traveled there to brief him and his personnel on plans to provide artillery support for their upcoming operation. He had been my group commander in Germany, and ten years later, he wrote a letter of support for my promotion to lieutenant colonel.

Cu Chi was and continues to be notorious for underground tunnels. Those tunnels are now a tourist attraction in the Cu Chi District of Ho Chi Minh City (Saigon). During the Vietnam War, the tunnels were the Viet Cong's base of operations for several campaigns to include the Tet Offensive in 1968. Apparently, the Viet Cong had a network of tunnels under much of the country. American soldiers who were small in stature were often given the task of entering those tunnels. They were referred to as "tunnel rats."

Anything could be found in those tunnels—hospitals, food and weapon caches, communications equipment, etc. Of course, the tunnels were often booby-trapped with concealed punji spikes and bamboo stakes, the tips of which were poisoned with buffalo dung. Soldiers stepping into wet areas would suddenly suffer a spike piercing their foot and the immediate onset of infection.

Drug use seemed high in Vietnam with many smoking marijuana, using psychedelics such as LSD, heroin, or other hard drugs. Again, I witnessed very little drug use in my units. Periodically, we saw a Vietnamese on the perimeter trying to sell drugs to the troops, but we conducted drug counseling often to preach the downsides of drug use. In fact, the battalion commander often sent troubled troops from other batteries to my unit in his effort to save them.

Many days and nights, I sat with my soldiers and reminded them of the downside of using drugs—receiving a "less than honorable" discharge from the Army and returning home to experience great difficulty finding adequate employment or pursuing military supported education. Honestly, I think I saved many young soldiers from that scenario. I cried and was very emotional when I mounted the helicopter leaving my troops to head home to America. Of course, my thoughts quickly turned to my waiting family. I prayed their new commander took great care of them.

I never bought into or seriously question why we were fighting in Vietnam. I was a soldier and I followed orders. One of the most prized possessions I had was my radio. I was able to hear American broadcasts (public radio, I suppose), and I occasionally listened to the broadcast of Hanoi Hannah, loud and clear. Hanoi Hannah was a Vietnamese lady who spoke in broken English, directing her comments directly at the American soldier. She often reported on events taking place in America such as the protests against the war. She attempted to make the American soldier question their mission in Vietnam.

A highlight during my tour was a visit by actress Martha Raye. She arrived in the afternoon, dressed in a camouflaged uniform, ate and talked with the troops, played cards and drank beer with them; she was a true blessing. I'll never forget her visit. I encourage the reader to do an internet search for Hanoi Hannah and Martha Raye for their involvement during the Vietnam War. I choose not to, so as not to taint my memory of the events.

Departure from Vietnam, September 2, 1967

Based on my performance of duty in Vietnam, I was awarded the Bronze Star Medal for meritorious service in connection with military operations against a hostile force for the period June 1966 to September 1967. My preparation training time at Fort Irwin, California, was included in the span for the award.

Years after my Vietnam experience, I often wondered why the two units I commanded were spared the major enemy attacks and why not one soldier under my command was wounded or killed. First, I praise God. Second, when we relocated to a new area, we always sought out the local village leaders. If we identified a need our unit could fulfill, we attempted to do so.

For instance, my cooks often provided excess c-rations, my medics bandaged minor wounds and dispensed antibiotics by pill or needle if needed, and my first sergeant kept the soldiers away from the girls as much as possible. We all provided candy and desserts to the kids. Wherever we were located, it was virtually impossible to distinguish the enemy from the friendly villagers. We never really knew the difference. I have always felt our friendly approach to the surrounding villagers contributed to our safety. On more than one occasion, units that arrived after our relocation suffered enemy attacks and casualties.

Chapter 11

Assignment to Syracuse University

When I returned from Vietnam in 1967, I didn't receive a big welcome home from my country. At that time, protesters were burning the American flag and draft cards. My family more than made up with their warm welcome. For more than forty years, I seldom talked about serving in Vietnam, not only because of Post-Traumatic Stress Disorder (PTSD) but because I didn't think people appreciated my service. Today, when I wear Vietnam paraphernalia, persons I meet in the street are most gracious in expressing their sincere appreciation for my service. Their comments are deeply appreciated.

Field Artillery Officer Advanced Course, Fort Sill, Oklahoma, October 1967

I was assigned to Fort Sill, Oklahoma, to attend the Field Artillery Officer Advanced Course. My oldest son, Clifton, had begun his first year of school in Virginia. My father (his granddad) was there to see him get on the school bus for the first time. Living with his granddad for my first tour in Vietnam certainly cemented their special relationship.

We lived off-post in Lawton, Oklahoma. Clifton Jr. had to continue his first year of school in a new environment because we had moved from Virginia to Oklahoma. I hadn't given much thought to the fact that Clifton Jr.'s first school experience took him from an all-Black environment (teachers and students) to an integrated school environment. At six years old, he probably never gave it any thought.

At the end of his first year, his teacher informed us she didn't think he was mature enough to be promoted to the second grade. He had a habit of sitting on his legs in his chair. Well, this was our first child. We took the opinion of the teacher and had Clifton repeat the first grade.

We determined later that it was a major mistake on our part. Clifton had no problem with future schooling. Years later, I couldn't believe I witnessed an executive-level gentleman sitting on his legs in his office chair at Fort Monroe. I said to myself, "How dumb was I to hold my son back for that reason."

After my return home from Vietnam but before beginning my classes in the Field Artillery Officer Advanced Course, I suffered severe headaches to the point of being hospitalized at the Fort Sill military hospital for several days. Doctors determined the cause to be sinusitis and residual stress following my year in combat.

The Field Artillery Officer Advanced Course was eight months long, ending October 15, 1968. I graduated on the Commandant's List. While there, I was promoted to major.

Assignment to Syracuse University as a Major, November 11, 1968–May 21, 1971

Upon graduation, I was assigned to Syracuse University as an Assistant Professor of Military Science on the Reserve Officers Training Corps (ROTC) staff.

When we first arrived in Syracuse, New York, we were provided with family housing on Hancock Field, a small air force base. Later, we moved into a nice civilian home at 104 Candee Avenue, Syracuse, New York. It was an older house and very difficult to maintain. Finally, we relocated to a townhouse in Hollywood Park, Liverpool, New York, a suburb of Syracuse.

That's when we met Robert and Dorothy Adams. Over the years, Robert became one of my best friends. He and I had a strong love for the wonders of mathematics and spent a lot of time discussing various concepts. Robert, "Rabbit" to me, was employed as a computer engineer at the General Electric Company Computer Division, and Dorothy was a secondary school teacher.

Syracuse is in the Snowbelt. It snowed in October, and we didn't see the ground until April. However, the city had the equipment to keep roads open. We didn't miss any time from work or school. Often the snow was piled so high we couldn't see houses.

It was a wonderful assignment for the family. There was much to do. We secured a popup camper from Hancock Field and took off for the Adirondacks, Poconos, and Catskill Mountain areas to soak in nature's beauty. The kids enjoyed roughing it in the popup camper and pup tents.

We couldn't afford expensive vacations or fancy clothes, but we managed and were happy. Viola and I did manage to take a cruise to Alaska and had a great time in Ketchikan, Sitka, and Juneau. In Skagway, we took an uphill train ride to enjoy an overlook of the Yukon Valley made famous by the television show *Sergeant Preston of the Yukon*. Viola chose not to participate in the next adventure, but I took a helicopter trip to tour the ice glaciers. We landed on a glacier. With special non-slip shoes, we were encouraged to debark the helicopter and walk around. The glacier wasn't level, and there were splits in the creaking ice. We weren't provided a rope or lifeline to hang onto. As I wandered close to a crevice in the ice, I couldn't see the bottom and actually froze in fear. I had to be escorted back to the helicopter by the pilot.

On one occasion, Viola's parents visited, and we traveled to Montreal, Canada, to attend the World Fair, "Man in His World." On the return trip home to Syracuse during a heavy downpour of rain, I witnessed something I'd never seen before. It appeared to be raining frogs. Of course, I know better, but there were hundreds of frogs on the highway.

My parents and brother Lafayette visited us while we resided in Liverpool. I don't remember what we did to entertain them, but I do remember giving Lafayette my 1957 Thunderbird convertible as he began his freshman year at Norfolk State University. That car, with its 400+ cubic inch engine, could squeal tires for half a block. Lafayette kept the vehicle for at least four years while in college at Norfolk State University.

I will always cherish the memory of Clifton Jr. participating in the Cub Scouts. He and I made a car to compete in the Pinewood Derby. Major William Knapp, a fellow member of the ROTC office, was a native of Syracuse and had snowmobiles at his parents' home. When we took them out, we had to carefully avoid running into fences because the height of the snow often hid them.

Being on a college campus in a military uniform during the Vietnam War was quite an experience. First of all, the anti-Vietnam movement was the main attraction in the news media. Universities such as Cornell, fifty-two miles down the road, shut down their ROTC programs. Even those institutions retaining the program dictated various restrictions on the ROTC staff, i.e., no wearing of military uniforms or using military vehicles on campus. None of those restrictions were ever placed on our program at Syracuse University. There were pickets and demonstrations on campuses all over America. Syracuse University had dissident students on campus who occupied the ROTC offices for three days. Later, on my annual evaluation, my supervisor wrote:

> Major Collins works well under pressure in addition to his excellence in the more prosaic aspects of his duties. For example, during the student disturbances of last year, he was a tower of strength when the ROTC offices were occupied for a period of three days. Calm, rational, and able to communicate with the students, he was particularly effective in keeping control of a situation that had an ominous potential for disaster.

The dissident student representatives were allowed to vent their frustrations and complaints. I will always remember a highly vocal student leader who I talked with for hours about the pros and cons of the Vietnam War, but most importantly, why our presence on campus had nothing to do with the war.

Teaching ROTC classes was a joy. ROTC participation wasn't mandatory; therefore, the students who chose to join were eager to attend the classes. The many duties assigned during my tour at Syracuse University included advisor to freshman and senior cadets, adjutant, cadet administrative officer, commandant of cadets, operations and training officer, flight training coordinator, and rifle team advisor. I prepared, supervised, and in part, presented instruction for the four-year ROTC program. I also coordinated and directed the ROTC scholarship and awards programs.

A truly blessed moment was when I appeared before the University Senate Curriculum Committee, representing eighteen colleges/schools, to obtain university sponsorship and approval for academic credit of my military science course, World Change and Military Implications. In other words, any student, ROTC cadet or not, could take my course for academic credit. That was the first time an ROTC course had been accepted for sponsorship by the university as part of courses available to all students.

My entire three-year assignment took place during the Vietnam War. The ROTC detachment was given the task of providing Next of Kin (NOK) and Survivor Assistance Officer (SAO) services to the surrounding areas. In other words, when a soldier was reported missing or killed in action, an Army officer from our detachment was tasked to notify the family within four hours. Well, guess who was given the assignment on many occasions during my three-year tour?

Can you imagine driving fifty miles into the countryside where there probably were no military personnel within twenty-five miles, pulling into the driveway, and walking to the front door in full military uniform to inform a wife and/or family their loved one had been declared missing or killed in combat? Some recipients simply broke down in tears. Some got outright angry. Families often declared me a liar, threatened bodily harm to me, or threatened to get a gun. At times, I had to leave my card and return with another officer.

During the time of war, or even today with continuing combat around the world, it's traumatic when a military sedan pulls into a driveway, and military personnel approach the door. I can only imagine that feeling, knowing a loved one is either missing or dead. On one occasion, when I reached the home, the deceased soldier's mother and father were there, but the soldier's wife was working several miles away at the local Sears Roebuck Store. I had to sit in the parlor with the mother while the father traveled to bring the wife home. Then and only then could I inform the deceased soldier's mother and father—in the presence of the wife—of my purpose for being there. That was a tough one.

Eventually, I decided to always take a minister, rabbi, or priest with me for NOK assignments. The SAO assignments were not as bad. Once the family had been notified by the NOK officer, then an SAO was assigned to assist the family in making funeral arrangements and ensure they received all their survivor benefits.

Our sixth child, Michael, was born in Syracuse in March 1970. We then had six kids, ages nine, eight, six, four, four, and a newborn.

Viola and I had our hands full. Dorothy and Robert Adams did a lot to help us care for the kids. Of course, I never shied away from trying to do as much or more than Viola, including changing diapers, bathing them, feeding them, etc. My biggest challenge was to budget my income to cover the care of the family. During our forty-one years of marriage, I never attempted to pursue a second job, except on the one occasion I spoke of earlier. I believed my presence in the home to help take care of the kids and spend time with the family was more important than securing additional income.

Every summer, the ROTC staff accompanied the cadets to summer camp at Fort Indiantown Gap military reservation located in Lebanon County, Pennsylvania. Clifton Jr. was eight years old and accompanied me for one week. Most officers desired to be assigned as a cadet company commander, a career-enhancing position. The major drawback to that assignment was I would have to be away from my family for the entire six-week camp. I chose not to fight for a command position but instead ran a target acquisition or a rifle range. The key to my choice of assignments was the ranges were only operational Tuesday through Thursday. Therefore, I departed for home every Thursday evening and returned to Fort Indiantown Gap by six o'clock Tuesday morning in time to open the range. That gave me plenty of time with my family. Praise the Lord, my vehicle quit on me only one time, and I had to thumb a ride half the way down Interstate 81.

During the summer of 1969, I was in charge of four target detection ranges on which 5,900 cadets were trained. The cadets were seated in bleachers with grass, brush, and trees to their front. My staff were dressed in camouflage outfits and painted faces to preclude detection as they worked their way toward the bleachers. The aim was to get closer and closer to the cadets without being detected. Once my personnel were detected, the cadets were in shock as to their closeness. I then trained the cadets on the effective detection of an enemy.

To detect movement, focus on an object directly in front of you. If anything moves anywhere within your peripheral vision, you will detect the movement. The mistake most people make is to continuously scan an area. When scanning, movement is nearly impossible to detect.

At the 1970 ROTC Advanced Summer Camp, I was the Officer-in-Charge and Principal Instructor at Trainfire Range 11 where more than 5,900 cadets were required to detect and engage targets as they popped up down range. At that time, the M14 with a twenty-round magazine was the weapon employed by the U.S. Army. Midway during the Vietnam War, the M14 was replaced by the M16. Both weapons were considered inferior to the Russian developed AK47 provided and used by the North Vietnamese and Viet Cong soldiers. U.S. Army Special Forces and U.S. Navy SEAL Teams used the captured AK47s in Vietnam.

While assigned to Syracuse University and ten years into my military career, IBM almost recruited me. In the late 1960s, large companies were encouraged to employ personnel of color to secure federal contracts. Ten years of military service, Black, and with a mathematics degree made me a prime prospect. An IBM recruiter visited campus and offered me an IBM sales job with an annual salary of $18,000 plus commission on my future sales. It was a fantastic salary arrangement at that time. Even after my negative response, he requested I accompany him to the airport for further discussion.

Although the offer was enticing, several things were uppermost on my mind. First, I had a wife and five kids (at that time) who needed my presence.

The IBM position required constant travel away from my family. Also, I had only ten more years to stay in the military to earn a lifetime retirement income and continued full medical coverage for my wife and children. It was too much to give up. However, I had no idea I would be sent back to combat in Vietnam the next year.

On my departure from Syracuse University, I was awarded the Meritorious Service Medal.

Chapter 12

Second Deployment to Vietnam

After serving one tour in Vietnam, I thought that was it. Well, the Army felt differently, for I was put on orders to serve a second tour in May 1971. I'll never understand, for there were officers who were never sent to Vietnam and certainly not a second time. Had it been possible, I would have gotten out of the Army. But, once on orders, I couldn't say no. I was leaving behind my wife and six children, ages ten, nine, seven, five, five, and one.

Viola Collins and our six kids on an outing, circa 1973

Viola and the kids moved into a home we purchased on Tweed Road in Richmond, Virginia. Fortunately, Viola had grown up in Richmond and her family still resided there. In fact, her sister Jackey moved in and was a great help to her. I still marvel at the fact Viola did such a magnificent job raising the kids and managing the home during my absence. She was not raised with sisters and brothers. Much of our family dynamics were rather foreign to her. At least I was raised with sisters and brothers, so I was familiar with sibling squabbles. The outstanding outcome of our kids is indeed a testament to her effectiveness as a mother.

My second tour in Vietnam was a walk in the park compared to my first tour. I had hot meals, a shower, and a clean dry bed almost every day. I was assigned as the Plans Officer of the Qui Nhon Sub-Area Command, a major maintenance, supply, service, and transportation organization. There were other support commands in Saigon, Cam Ranh Bay, and later in Da Nang. Each support command operated independently in maintaining a flow of needed goods to the combat zones.

The living conditions were much better than my previous tour, and we were inside buildings. The unit headquarters was located in a gated compound located within the city limits of Qui Nhon. Most facilities within the compound were large stucco buildings.

Our sleeping quarters were in a one-story square-shaped motel-style compound with a grassy court area. The inner court was surrounded by sandbags, and motel-style rooms circled the court. Each room had an elevated bunk bed high enough to crawl under during enemy activity. A row of sandbags in the center of the room provided some safety from incoming rockets or mortars. When alerted, we crawled under the bunk beds and remained there until the all-clear was given.

Praise the Lord, we never received a direct hit. I made a covenant with God, if He got me out of Vietnam in one piece this second time, I would display a cross around my neck or lapel for the remainder of my life. Some people call that "Foxhole Christianity."

I was assigned to the security, plans and operations office supervised by Lieutenant Colonel (LTC) James S. Guyton. LTC Guyton was a tall, athletic, articulate, and confident Black gentleman who taught me a lot about the military. He took time to pass on certain tidbits he had learned about the system and how to take care of your career. I'll never forget those conversations. I mentored several young officers over the years echoing his guidance.

Major Clifton Collins Sr. at his desk, Qui Nhon, Republic of Vietnam, December 1971

On September 14, 2020, I managed to locate and talk with LTC Guyton. He was turning eighty-eight years old in a few days and sounded wonderful. The last time we talked was in 1972, forty-eight years ago in Vietnam. What a blessing! I was also reminded that he is my fraternity brother, a member of Kappa Alpha Psi Fraternity, Inc.

As LTC Guyton's plans officer, I prepared policies, plans, and programs pertaining to the organization and operational functions of seven battalion-type combat service support units, supervised the defense operations center, and performed functions of the staff signal officer. My staff had the primary mission of planning and coordinating the logistical support of nearly 50,000 Free World Military Forces in the northern portion of Military Region Two, Republic of Vietnam. During the war, South Vietnam was divided into four military regions or corps. To fulfill our mission, our command consisted of over 6,200 personnel with its main headquarters in Qui Nhon and seven battalions representing the functions of transportation, petroleum, oil lubricant, and supply located in the Chang Rang Valley area.

On a typical day, I visited the defense operations bunker around five a.m. to receive a briefing from my operations personnel on enemy activity in our area of operations during the night. I was particularly interested in enemy activity near Highway 19 from Qui Nhon to Pleiku. Based on intelligence, I contacted my supervisor, LTC Guyton, and recommended whether the daily supply convoys should be a go or no go, particularly to Pleiku.

If his decision was a go, a convoy of approximately ten to fifteen 5,000-gallon fuel tankers and other cargo vehicles departed at seven a.m. from the nearby Chang Rang Valley to make the round trip to Pleiku. The trip was one hundred miles long to Pleiku with the major concern of being ambushed, particularly while passing through the An Khe and Mang Yang Passes. The tankers were required to reach Pleiku, be off-loaded, and start the return trip to their home base, the Chang Rang Valley, no later than two p.m. We didn't want them to be on the road at night. The trip took a little over four hours each way due to the poor maintenance of the highway. Even today when I mapped the route, it's a three and a half-hour trip, suggesting that the highway has been upgraded slightly.

As the months passed in 1971, the command was given the order to phase out of Vietnam. Many of the combat units we supplied had departed Vietnam, and it became obvious the United States was beginning to disengage. I was assigned the task of writing the plan to get our entire command of over 6,200 personnel out of Vietnam over three to four months. I drafted the plan within twenty-four hours by spending the entire day and night doing so. It was approved by my supervisor and commander without any changes and approved by the commanding general at our higher headquarters at Cam Ranh Bay. LTC Guyton submitted a special efficiency report on me to the Headquarters of the Department of the Army in recognition of that and other accomplishments.

The "Reduction in Force" plan was classified and given the short title of RED Plan. In writing and executing the plan, I had to be mindful of our continuing mission while at the same time reducing the number of personnel and equipment in-country. I constantly implemented changes to various systems, procedures, information flows, supporter-supported relationships, inventory control, and stockpile.

Daily, I monitored the retention of the correct mixture of personnel and equipment to support other organizations. For example, if fifty vehicles were put on ships to be transported to Okinawa, South Korea, or the United States, perhaps fifty drivers, twenty-five mechanics, five cooks, and ten officers could depart Vietnam. I had to coordinate these actions not only with my organization commanders but also with U.S. contract civilians and representatives of the Vietnamese and Korean Army and Navy.

Another concern was the security of the docked ships waiting to be loaded. On occasions, Viet Cong sappers (persons who placed explosives on the hull of ships) managed to escape detection by underwater security measures and successfully blew holes in the hull of ships.

At least once a week, I traveled 150 miles by helicopter to Cam Ranh Bay to brief the higher headquarters on our troop/equipment reduction progress. Although there was a two-star general in the briefing room, the Black colonel present was the most impressive to me.

His name was Colonel Fred Clifton Sheffey Jr., a battalion commander who was later promoted to major general (two-star) and became the commanding general at Fort Lee, Virginia, in 1978. In my briefing, he appeared to command the room, and his presence was encouraging to me. His questions enhanced my presentations, and I felt encouraged on departure.

Once in the air for my return to Qui Nhon, a highlight for me was to have the pilot stopover in Nha Trang and land the helicopter at a U.S. Ranger Camp. From there, we borrowed a jeep and proceeded to a restaurant where they served huge lobsters. My second tour in Vietnam was nothing like the tours encountered by the fighting men in the jungles. My biggest fear was the constant threat of harm from shelling, ambushes, and attacks. I was not actually in the jungle searching for the enemy.

I don't remember the exact month I met Viola in Hawaii in early 1972 for a week of R and R (rest and recreation). The Army provided travel and hotel expenses for one week for wives to meet with their husbands traveling from Vietnam. There were several choices of locations in the far east, Bangkok, Hawaii, Tokyo, Hong Kong, etc. We chose Hawaii. All I can say is we had a ball. It was a wonderful week for both of us, being together for the sole purpose of loving each other. Regretfully, I had to return to the combat zone and send my wife back to care for our six kids.

During that same year, my grandmother (Dad's mom), Maggie "Peggie" Satchell died on April 16, 1972, at her home in Eastville, Virginia. My family contacted the Red Cross, and I was allowed to travel to the States to attend her funeral.

As part of the Reduction in Force Plan I had authored earlier, my command in Vietnam authorized a one-way trip home to attend my grandmother's funeral without having to return, cutting my second Vietnam tour to only eleven months.

Receiving Second Bronze Star Medal

Upon my departure from Vietnam, I was awarded my second Bronze Star Medal. Just as during my first tour in Vietnam, there were no casualties of personnel serving under my supervision during the second tour. Praise the Lord!

I'm thankful to God that, while in Vietnam, I never had to point a rifle or pistol at a human being. However, I realize my unit's 105mm howitzers probably killed a lot of people and is the main reason for my post-traumatic stress disorder (PTSD) diagnosis by the Veterans Administration. I live with the guilt of the unknown persons I may have killed. I often think back to the day I killed that innocent bird with my BB-gun.

Chapter 13

First Assignment to Fort Monroe, Virginia

In 1972, when I returned from Vietnam, I was assigned to Fort Monroe, Virginia. After commuting for several weeks from Richmond where I had left my family while in Vietnam, we moved as a family to Fort Monroe. My welcome home from Vietnam was again uneventful, and I didn't feel encouraged to broadcast the fact I was a returning Vietnam veteran.

One year later, the military draft was ended, and the United States Armed Forces moved to an all-volunteer military. The mandatory requirement for draft registration stopped in 1975. It was reinstated in 1980 after the Soviet invasion of Afghanistan. Every man between the ages of eighteen and twenty-five must now register with the Selective Service.

My opinion is every male should be subject to the draft. I also think much racial harmony results from persons of various races and ethnic groups being forced to live and work together for mutual survival. The current all-volunteer military allows congressional members and others to make decisions that may not affect them or their loved ones directly. Plus, I opine that a significant portion of volunteers are joining the armed forces as a last resort.

My Struggle with Panic Attacks

I suffered a lot of anxiety and guilt after my first tour in Vietnam to the point of considering suicide numerous times, something I never wanted to speak of to my family or anyone. In fact, my oldest son, Clifton Jr., only learned of my suicidal thoughts in 2018 when I was speaking to a Christian men's group at Fort Eustis, Virginia, concerning my Vietnam experience.

Of course, having to serve a second tour didn't help. Both of my tours were easy compared to what many troops endured, so I cannot imagine their struggles. Although I returned from the second combat tour in 1972, I was still being treated for panic anxiety in 1981 when I retired from the military nine years later. To this day, I can't view an R-rated movie with any amount of violence in it.

At one point during my treatment, I was prescribed the drug Xanax, which can become habit forming. Fearing the adverse effects of the drug, I decided to reduce the prescribed three tablets a day to one or, at the most, two tablets a day. Unfortunately, I still suffered major panic attacks at any time both day and night. For example, while sitting in church, I found myself suddenly breaking out in the biggest sweat, to the point of leaving the sanctuary to hide in the bathroom until I calmed down.

Many years ago while in college, I minored in physics and learned no two things can occupy the same space at the same time. Using this theorem, I managed to overcome many major problematic situations in my life. One night I suffered an attack, sweating profusely in my bed, and began to chant praises to God, "Praise the Lord, thank you, Jesus," over and over, until eventually, I calmed down and fell asleep. Since that night, I haven't taken any medication or suffered another attack. So, no two things can occupy the same space at the same time. Good will replace evil, love will replace hate, compliments will replace complaints, and good thoughts will replace bad thoughts.

Several years ago, I was evaluated at the Hampton Veteran Administration Center and ultimately diagnosed as suffering with Post-Traumatic Stress Disorder (PTSD).

Race Relations/Equal Opportunity and Equal Employment Opportunity

In 1971, the Department of Defense took action to end discrimination, and the Race Relations Institute was established. At that time, the Race Relations/Equal Opportunity (RR/EO) and Equal Employment Opportunity (EEO) programs for military and civilian personnel, respectively, began to take on increased significance within the Department of Defense. There was a big push by the military to bring about some semblance of good race relations and equal opportunity.

Many firsts came about. In 1971, Samuel L. Gravely became the first Black admiral in the history of the United States Navy. In 1972, Sergeant

Major Edgar R. Huff became the first Black to complete thirty years of service as a Marine. In 1974, five Black women were among the first group of female cadets at the Merchant Marine Academy. In 1975, Lieutenant Donna P. Davis became the first Black woman physician in the history of the Naval Medical Corps. Also in 1975, General Daniel "Chappie" James became the first Black four-star general in military history. However, in 1975, of more than 1,200 generals and admirals, there were only nineteen Blacks, less than 2 percent.

I was assigned to the Personnel Service Directorate. Initially, I was responsible for staff management of all Army personnel services programs conducted within the continental United States. These programs included RR/EO; EEO (covered federal civilian employees); Retirement Activities; Survivor Benefits; and Army Community Services. With the increased emphasis on race relations, the RR/EO and EEO programs became my total focus.

The RR/EO program focused on the military personnel side. My concept for staffing the entire U.S. Army Race Relations/Equal Opportunity program at all levels, to include the Army installations, was approved and implemented in 1973. My local RR/EO staff increased from three to sixteen personnel, and we managed the program for over 50,000 military and civilian personnel.

I authored the first United States Army Training and Doctrine Command Race Relations/Equal Opportunity Affirmative Action Plan (TRADOC RR/EO AAP). It was a thirty-seven-page document to create an environment of racial harmony and equal opportunity for every individual throughout the command. The document had to be coordinated with twenty-two agencies which required many briefings, conferences, and staff visits. The document was signed on April 5, 1974, by Commanding General William E. DePuy. I still have a copy of the original document.

On one occasion, I was directed to report to the office of the commanding general. Once there, General DePuy informed me there was racial unrest at Fort Benjamin Harrison, Indiana, and he directed me to investigate the situation. Once I arrived at Fort Harrison, I met with the installation race relations officer and was invited to a meeting of Black soldiers that evening.

After being accused of being pro-establishment, I was finally accepted and listened to their major complaint. I couldn't believe what I was hearing. In the dining hall, several NCOs (non-commissioned officers) were stationed around the wall to catch soldiers who left their dirty trays on the table. Both

Black and White soldiers were guilty, but the Black soldiers viewed the "standing around the wall" issue as being too prison-like.

To protest that situation, the Black soldiers were consuming their food and, on a signal, leaving their trays on the tables and departing simultaneously. I learned the reason for their defiance stemmed from the perception of being in prison. A simple solution was to cease having the NCOs standing on the wall. I visited and provided that simple solution to Major General Daniel French, the post commander, and I was on the next plane home.

As the EEO program manager for federal civilian employees, I interpreted and followed the dictates of federal regulations in the development of the first TRADOC EEO Plan of Action. The Plan of Action was briefed at every level of command, up to and including the Assistant Secretary of Defense where it was approved, and later used as a model for the total Army civilian workforce. The Plan of Action was designed to improve the economic, social, and educational opportunities for all civilian employees with particular emphasis on minorities and women. Specific milestones were developed and monitored throughout the command. Many staff visits were conducted to assess the effectiveness of EEO programs of subordinate commands. I take great pride in being a major force in the increased recognition received by EEO and the Federal Women's program during the early 1970s. In 1974, I was designated as the Equal Employment Opportunity Officer of the Year.

This quote is taken from my evaluation report: *It should be noted for the record that Major Collins has done more than any other officer in Hq TRADOC to promote racial harmony throughout the command.*

While assigned to Fort Monroe, we lived in Wherry housing for perhaps a year. We were assigned to a three-bedroom apartment along the Chesapeake Bay leading to the Officers' Club. When we walked out of our backdoor, we could walk twenty steps, cross the paved berm, and step into the water. The family often fished from the berm and cooked the catch on the grille in our backyard. We had a ball. The major drawback to that home was the lack of bedrooms for our family of eight. Therefore, our name was finally selected to move onto the main post into a second-floor four-bedroom apartment. Above the apartment was a finished attic. We converted the two-room attic into our family or party rooms. Our parents, relatives, and friends had a grand time in the attic. There was much dancing and partying.

Fort Monroe was a great place for the entire family. Being completely surrounded by water, there was only one gate onto the post. When we allowed the kids to ride their bikes and play outside, we didn't worry about them leaving the post. Fort Monroe couldn't be beat for fishing and crabbing. We fished from piers or anywhere along the mile-long berm. Crabbing was also a favorite. We used a flashlight to draw the crabs closer to our baited lines and then scooped them up with the long-handled nets. We also had crab cages baited with chicken necks. When the crabs followed the light to the cage, we pulled them up, trapping the poor crabs.

Military Branch Transfer

In 1972, I received a letter from the Department of Army stating there were too many field artillery officers on active duty, and I had three choices: 1) continue to serve in the Field Artillery Branch, 2) accept a three-year branch transfer to another branch, or 3) accept a permanent transfer to another branch.

I saw the handwriting on the wall. Since swelling to a Vietnam peak of 1.4 million men in 1968, the Army eventually trimmed back to 772,000 members, including a loss of 2,500 officers. If I remained in the Field Artillery Branch, I was likely to be discharged from the military very soon, forfeiting military retirement eligibility.

At that time, I had been in the military for twelve years and I needed a total of eighteen years to be locked in for military retirement. The letter provided a list of several branches with officer shortages for which I was deemed qualified. The Adjutant General (AG) Branch was one of the branches offered. Rather than taking the chance of being discharged prior to retirement eligibility, I chose to accept a branch transfer to AG Branch on March 2, 1973.

That branch encompassed personnel and administration and a high probability of working in an office atmosphere. Having been in field artillery for twelve years, I had gotten tired of being exposed to adverse weather, sleeping on the ground, placed in the midst of some forest (often in snow), and under other uncomfortable conditions. An office-type atmosphere in the AG Branch sounded good to me.

Well, it turned out to be a great decision. For the balance of my nine years in the military, I never really had a true AG position. However, my assignments and duties were now in an office type environment, and most importantly, I received my promotion.

Unfortunately, two of my close friends chose to stay in the over-strength Field Artillery Branch and were later cut from the Army prior to reaching retirement eligibility. One of the officers had served over seventeen years when he was informed his services were no longer needed and he had ninety days to get out. That deadline was exactly twenty-six days before he had completed eighteen years of active duty, an anniversary which would have locked him in the Army for twenty years and a life-long retirement with numerous benefits, including 50 percent of his salary. He fought his case in court to no avail.

After the branch transfer, I was sent to the AG School at Fort Benjamin Harrison in 1974 to attend a specially designed eight-week transition course for branch transferees. I graduated second in my class of thirty-three students, missing the top spot by 0.4 of a point (97.6 vs 98.0).

After *several years* had passed and I had been promoted to major, I felt a specific efficiency report I had received in Germany was going to lessen my probability of being promoted to lieutenant colonel. I wrote a letter to then-Lieutenant General (three-star) Fillmore K. Mearns, refreshed his memory of our association in Germany, and requested his assistance. I provided him with copies of my more recent records covering the period since we had served together. He responded by writing a letter to the Adjutant General of the Department of Army who oversees promotions. I am sure his letter had a significant impact on my promotion to lieutenant colonel. After ten plus years, he could have easily claimed lack of memory due to timespan and declined my request, but he didn't and I'm grateful.

Below is his letter.

Beaufort, S. C.
16 March 1976
Subject: Efficiency Rating, Clifton E. Collins,
     XXX-XX-XXXX, Major, AGC.

To: The Adjutant General,
     Department of Army,
     Washington, D. C.   20315

Major Collins has requested a letter from me on his behalf because he has been advised that efficiency reports for the period 12 Jan 65 – 26 Apr 66 are considered by Dept of Army to be adverse and may contribute to his non-selection to grade of lieutenant colonel. During the cited period, I was the reviewing officer.

In my opinion, Major Collins is a victim of poor judgement by rating and indorsing officers during the period in question. He is also the victim of an organizational blunder which eliminated the Target Acquisition Battalion echelon from each of the US Corps in USAREUR. In lieu of the battalion, two separate batteries were authorized. The latter action created an unwise and nearly intolerable command burden for separate Target Acquisition Battery Commanders. This situation exceeded a reasonable expectation for a young officer to perform with top quality results. My action taken on 26 Aug 65 as reviewing officer reflects those views but obviously was inadequate because the injustice of judgmental and organizational errors has lingered on to mar this officer's career. His subsequent efficiency reports show a consistently high-quality performance, and this entirely justifies my faith in this officer's ability and moral fiber.

My intervention on 26 Aug 65 had a basis in circumstances as cited in the first paragraph of my comment. There was no such circumstance when I reviewed the report ending on 26 Apr 66. My only alternative was to repudiate the judgement of two of my senior commanders.

At that time there was no basis for such action. In view of Major Collins' subsequent performance, I believe now that the judgements of Colonel Cline and of Colonel Cabaniss were faulty. The same applies to my own judgement.

I recommend that the reports in question not be considered in evaluating Major Collins' qualifications for promotion now nor in subsequent personnel actions regarding this officer.

F. K. Mearns
Lieut. General, US Army, Ret

I was promoted to lieutenant colonel six months later on November 12, 1976, and had a big promotion party at Fort Knox. I contacted and thanked General Mearns. His letter meant the world to me, not only for my Army career but also for my faith in people. I learned that General Mearns died six years later on November 18, 1997 at the age of eighty-two.

Lieutenant Colonel Clifton Collins Sr, 1976

Chapter 14

Assignment to Fort Knox, Kentucky

Soon after graduation from AG School, I was transferred to Fort Knox in November 1974, supposedly to be the Installation Adjutant General responsible for managing the personnel and administrative policies of the installation. Well, apparently that was not to be. Perhaps I'm being paranoid, but I have always felt the responsibility of managing the personnel and administrative policies of that major installation was not going to be given to a branch transferee. So, upon my arrival at Fort Knox, instead of assigning me to the adjutant general position, they had to find something for me to do.

I was given the task of analyzing and solving major management and control problems in the post family housing program. At that time, Fort Knox had the largest military family housing operation in the nation consisting of 4,276 homes. There were many maintenance complaints and much controversy concerning the housing assignment and waiting list policies. As a direct result of my analysis, the occupancy rate increased from 91 to 98 percent and the maintenance downtime was reduced by 71 percent. The number of complaints was drastically reduced, and the government saved several hundred thousand dollars. As usual, I went about doing the best job I could for about four months and was highly commended for a job well done.

Deputy Chief of Staff for Recruiting

Subsequently, the position of Deputy Chief of Staff for Recruiting (DCS-R) became vacant, and I was placed in that position. For career advancement, the Adjutant General position on an installation was ideal and preferred, however, the DCS-R position had its merits as well. For the non-military readers, an Army installation is normally commanded by a two-star general and managed by a colonel as the chief of staff.

As the DCS-R, I was rated by the chief of staff and endorsed by the commanding general. My job was to support every Army recruiter in every little town within the ten-state area surrounding Fort Knox. At that time, the Army had the Station of Choice and Unit of Choice recruiting programs. In other words, installations and major units were responsible for recruiting the personnel they needed to carry out their mission. For example, if the 194th Armored Brigade at Fort Knox anticipated the future need for twenty-four cooks and thirty-five drivers, the recruiters in the ten-state area were informed and given the mission of acquiring those personnel. More than 23,000 military personnel were assigned to Fort Knox in over 300 different skills. The dynamics of personnel management in that military environment necessitated the acquisition of nearly 500 new soldiers in the correct skills per month.

To assist those recruiters as the DCS-R, I had a staff of fourteen full-time military and civilian personnel, plus 140 auxiliary personnel. The auxiliary personnel included a mobile exhibit team that toured the ten-state area and 120 recruiter aides assigned to various geographical areas. The recruiter aides were soldiers who had graduated from advanced individual training at Fort Knox and been chosen to return to their home area to assist the local recruiter in recruiting others. The in-house staff included a civilian secretary, several senior non-commission officers, a six-member band, and other enlisted personnel to carry out the mission of supporting the recruiters.

As DCS-R, I also had the authority of acquiring personnel and/or equipment at Fort Knox to carry out our mission. For example, if an Army recruiter requested an on-site display of an Army helicopter and tank at a high school football game, or a band at a high school dance, or an Army vehicle to participate in a local parade, my office made it happen. During my three-year assignment, we recruited over 16,000 personnel from primarily the ten-state area, an increase of nearly 100 percent.

I noted a significant number of newly recruited personnel were being discharged soon after arrival for medical reasons. This was a huge cost to the Army to lose these individuals one to three days after enlisting, processing, and being shipped to the training centers. I visited several Military Enlistment Processing Centers including Louisville, Detroit, Chicago, and Saint Louis and followed the intake process from six in the morning when the young men checked in until they were declared qualified or not. The major causative factor turned out to be the lack of competency of the examining doctors. In other words, virtually all of the examiners were elderly retired doctors, often with personal mobility challenges. The required close examination of the unclothed recruits was not happening.

A great example was a young man who had lost a kidney. Well, if the doctor didn't notice the scar, he missed that fact and allowed the recruit into the training pipeline to be discharged later when he failed the challenge of basic training. Anyway, my report results tightened up the process and the incidents were drastically reduced, saving money. In fact, my report was used as my major paper when I was fulfilling my master's degree requirements.

Whenever our band was requested to support a high school function, we were required to ensure we had cleared our participation with all local bands in the high school area. Our band performance was at no cost to the high school, but we were not allowed to cause lost revenue for the local bands. Deployment of the six-man band was also a challenge; there were occasions of band member involvement with the high school female students. I made it very clear that fraternization with high school students would be severely punished. Of course, I was naïve to think it didn't happen, but I never had to discipline any band member.

I'm reminded of an event that gained me the nickname of "turkey man." We received the request to have a helicopter land on a high school football field during halftime. The mission appeared to have gone very well, and the Army recruiter and high school officials were happy. A week later, we received a letter stating the helicopter flight path had been over a turkey farm and had resulted in the death of many turkeys. Apparently, the noise overhead had frightened the turkeys so badly they flocked to a corner of their pen and many were smothered to death. Well, needless to say, the Army paid for those turkeys.

Throughout the country, influential civilians were selected and designated as Civilian Aides (CA) to the Secretary of the Army. The groups were composed of civilians from all specialties—medical, business, education, etc. Their primary focus was to learn as much as possible about the Army and support the Army recruiting programs in their communities. As the DCS-R, I served as the escort for the various CA groups visiting Fort Knox and demonstrated that the United States Army is a highly professional organization. I arranged for them to visit troop activities throughout the installation, classroom training, firing ranges, and tank training exercises.

Fort Knox was a wonderful assignment for the family. One of the housing areas on the post had perhaps twenty-five two-bedroom duplexes where the center wall had been removed to convert them to four-bedroom single homes. To qualify to live in those homes required a family of at least four children. Consequently, my kids had many, many potential playmates. Those who come to mind are the Kirksey, Quickmire, and Johnson families.

On the Fort Knox post, there was an elementary school, a high school, two bowling alleys, several swimming pools, a golf course, bank, commissary, post exchange, etc. Our home had four rooms in the basement. In one room, we had a wonderful train set with many make-believe train stations, towns, and forest areas. In the next room, we had a ping pong table. In the third room, we had a pool table. Finally, room number four was a spare bedroom. We allowed visiting foreign military students to occupy that room most of the time. With many playmates and activities, the family enjoyed Fort Knox.

During our tour, we took a couple of trips to Walt Disney World and water parks. We also took the kids on a couple Disney cruise ships.

While at Fort Knox, I managed to get a Master of Science in Systems Management Degree in an on-base program offered by the University of Southern California (USC) in 1978. The USC instructors arrived from the main campus, lived locally for the length of two courses, and then were replaced by new instructors for the next two courses. Being my own boss, I could close my office door during low periods and study.

I was also selected for the Honorable Order of Kentucky Colonels in 1977. Among other benefits, being a Kentucky Colonel automatically got me an invite to the governor's home for the annual cookout on the day before the Kentucky Derby. I never attended that function. Of course, they expected a donation from time to time. Receiving none, I eventually stopped receiving invitations (smile).

Since I had completed consecutive stateside assignments at Fort Monroe and Fort Knox, I was destined for an overseas assignment, probably Korea. Anticipating an undesirable assignment, I contacted the aide to General Donn Starry who had been my commander at Fort Knox as a two-star General. General Starry had now earned his fourth star and was the commanding general of the Training and Doctrine Command (TRADOC) at Fort Monroe. I informed his aide that my aging parents were on the Virginia Eastern Shore, and I wanted to return to Fort Monroe in lieu of an overseas assignment. In other words, I asked General Starry to use his influence with the Headquarters Department of the Army assignment office to get me back to Fort Monroe and not overseas. Soon thereafter, I received orders to return to Fort Monroe, Virginia, in 1977.

Chapter 15

Second Assignment to Fort Monroe, Virginia

When I returned to Fort Monroe for my second tour, guess what position I was slotted for? The Race Relations/ Equal Opportunity (RR/EO) position, with a civilian manager handling the Equal Opportunity Officer (EEO) program. When the division chief informed me I was going to pick up where I left off three years before, I simply informed him I had paid my dues in those programs and didn't wish to put myself or my family through that again. Of course, he was upset and informed me he had never had someone outright refuse to accept an assignment. Apparently, he knew I was serious and told me to wait at home until he could find me another position.

Junior Reserve Officers' Training Corps, September 1977

Earlier I stated that during my first tour at Fort Monroe, I had been the RR/EEO manager for military personnel as well as EEO manager for civilian personnel. Almost daily, I arrived home angry about some form of injustice that had come to my knowledge that day. It affected my outlook on life in general.

Two weeks later, I received a call informing me a position to supervise the Junior Reserve Officers' Training Corps (JROTC) Branch within the Cadet Command was available. Was I interested? I answered in the affirmative and reported to that office for duty.

As chief of the JROTC Branch for over four years, I provided staff supervision over the U.S. Army JROTC program conducted in 679 high schools throughout the United States and overseas with a staff of 1,600 personnel, a student body of 106,000 cadets, and a $19 million budget. Generally, my responsibilities included the development, interpretation, and implementation of policy; evaluation and selection of new high schools to host JROTC units; establishment, evaluation, and disestablishment of units; administration of cadet and instructor personnel; justification and monitorship of the budget; development of program of instruction and curriculum; administration of awards, decorations, and uniform policy; and maintenance and monitorship of the contractual agreement between the Army and host schools.

During my assignment, I was required to communicate within the military arena as well as with students, parents, and administrators of high schools throughout the world, members of the state and national legislative bodies, and others. Units were located in high schools in forty-one states and overseas (Guam, Samoa, Canal Zone, Virgin Islands, and Puerto Rico).

When I entered into my new assignment, I noted the program was somewhat outdated. Basically, there were two civilian ladies (Rita McGuire and Shirley Kirkland) doing the best they could to merely keep up with the daily requirements. The military supervisor had departed some months earlier. The ladies were performing yeoman work, and I immediately deemed them to be under graded with a civilian General Schedule pay grade of 5 (GS-5). It took me over a year, but I eventually managed to get them upgraded to GS-7.

After Vietnam, not only was the Army force being reduced, but there was an ongoing effort in Congress to reduce the number of high schools hosting the Junior ROTC program. We had hundreds of applications from high schools wanting to establish the program in their schools. By developing and applying a combination of statistical and mathematical techniques (primarily linear regression equations), I was capable of predicting and consummating the equitable distribution of units and could readily justify each selection objectively.

Once members of Congress and others were provided information on the selection methodology, inquiries relating to non-selection of schools were virtually nonexistent. Not only did the ladies and I revamp the application criteria and procedures, but we developed a survey that was sent to every high school hosting the JROTC program. Based on data gathered, I sent a report to Congressman Ike Skelton of Missouri reflecting that more than 50 percent of JROTC graduates continued their affiliation with the military by entering military academies, joining a military service, or enrolling in the ROTC program at a college. Congressman Skelton was the chairman of the House Armed Services Committee. Because those statistics proved the worthiness of the JROTC program to the overall military recruiting efforts, the pending reductions were reversed and authorization for 190 additional units was granted.

Additionally, I was the principal author of over 1,300 pages of instructional material (four textbooks) developed for the JROTC program, which was highly commended by students and school officials around the world.

Another achievement I am extremely blessed to have played a part in was the establishment of the Franklin Military Academy in Richmond, Virginia, in 1980. In public high schools, Junior ROTC enrollment has always been voluntary. To counter disciplinary challenges, the Richmond school district requested the establishment of a Junior ROTC program in an unoccupied facility wherein all student enrollees were required to enroll in the Junior ROTC program. This was going to be a first. I visited and met with school officials at the facility and, after a thorough inspection, deemed the facility to be adequate to host the program. Of course, one of the main requirements was security of military weapons. To my knowledge, the Franklin Military Academy is the only public high school in the nation where every attendee must enroll in the Junior ROTC program.

As an aside, my office managed to establish the first JROTC unit in the state of New Jersey and the Republic of South Korea in 1981.

Life has its wonders. Throughout my military career, I was blessed to run into many of my college classmates. My replacement as chief of the JROTC branch was Lieutenant Colonel Donald Miles (deceased), a classmate from Virginia State University.

Throughout my military career, I had challenges passing the annual physical fitness test. I could do the pushups, the chin-ups, run around the obstacles, and crawl, but I always had trouble passing the two-mile run. Being a chain-smoker and overweight didn't help. I struggled and completed the run, but the scale doesn't lie (smile). I have always said the Army had the wrong weight standard for people like me. I am six feet two inches tall, however, the inseam of my pants is only thirty-one inches. In other words, I have an unusually long torso and short legs. The Army had a weight limit of 216 pounds for my height, and I often weighed 230 plus. I was always in a weight reduction program.

Retirement from the Army, December 1981

Upon my retirement from the military in December 1981, I was awarded the Legion of Merit, one of only two decorations to be issued by the military as neckwear, the other being the Medal of Honor. My service in Vietnam reaped two Bronze Star Medals, the National Defense Service Medal, Vietnam Campaign Medal, and the Vietnam Cross of Gallantry w/Palm. Two Meritorious Service Medals were earned while at Syracuse University and Fort Knox, and there were numerous other military awards of distinction.

I thought it would be worthy of note that while serving for twenty-one years in the military, my family lived in eighteen different houses. Needless to say, they certainly had a wide variety of friends, social environments, school systems, and heartbreak. I know it must have been difficult to constantly leave certain friends and situations. I praise the Lord my children are all wonderful grownups now.

At the time of my military retirement, three of our children were in college: Clifton Jr. at Hampton University, Sharon at Old Dominion University, and Janice at Wake Forest University. Later, Ronald and Donald attended Morgan State University and Michael attended Norfolk State University. All of them attained their college degrees and some achieved postgraduate degrees. All of the boys served in the Armed Forces.

I regret not participating in the retirement ceremony at Fort Monroe offered by Headquarters, United States Training and Doctrine Command. The retirement ceremonies were quite a spectacular event with a marching band, troop units, state and local dignitaries, followed by a nice reception at the Officers' Club. My wife, kids, parents, other family members, work associates, and many others would have enjoyed the experience. That was shamefully selfish on my part, for to me, it was not a big thing. I was somewhat bitter about the unfairness of the system that I had given twenty-one years of my life, and I had to fight for fairness every day.

I had not given it much thought, but normal school life for a kid involves three schools: elementary, middle, and high school. However, during my military career, my kids were required to endure at least ten different schools. An example involved my last military assignment at Fort Monroe. We lived in the Carybrook area of Hampton, then moved on post at Fort Monroe, followed by the purchase of our home in Hampton. The kids were required to change schools during each relocation. Considering the constant requirement to leave friends and make new friends, my kids were and are magnificent.

Military Retirement, December 1981. Beginning in the rear from left to right: Maggie (mother), Clifton (dad), Serena Harmon (mid-wife). Second row: Emma Bryant (aunt), Janice (daughter), Donald (Son). Third row: Ronald (son), Clifton, Jr. (son), Sharon (daughter), Barbara (sister), Herman Eure (brother-in-law). Fourth row: Lauren (niece), Jared (nephew). Front row: Michael (son), Viola, Clifton

Chapter 16

Return to Civilian Life

Viola and I decided to remain in the Hampton Roads area. Had we wanted to move within a year after my retirement, the military would have paid for our relocation anywhere within the continental United States. We decided that Fort Monroe/Hampton, Virginia area was, once again, a wonderful place to live. There was a bunch of things for the family to do—close to the water, not far from the mountains, near the visitor mecca of Washington D.C., not far from the southern charm of the Carolinas, as well as the wonderful diversity of four weather seasons.

All six of our kids were either in high school or college. To top it all off, it was about an hour drive west to Viola's family in Richmond and an hour east to my family on the Eastern Shore. The kids were ages eleven, fifteen, fifteen, seventeen, nineteen, and twenty and had a wealth of activities to keep them occupied.

We managed to take family vacations as often as possible, considering the expense of eight people. Viola and I often sat at the table in our pretty 1977 Chevrolet van parked in the driveway and listened to music while sipping wine. The van, with its decorative exterior, large bay windows, strobe lights around the ceiling, swivel seats, and removable table in the center was set up for a good time.

While moving around during my military career, Viola took courses at Elizabethtown Community College in Kentucky and Thomas Nelson Community College in Hampton, Virginia. If my memory is correct, Viola's first job was as a bank teller in Syracuse, New York, when I was serving as a ROTC instructor at Syracuse University between 1968 and 1971. Later, she worked for the federal government at Fort Knox, Kentucky from 1974 to 1977. When we left Fort Knox for my assignment to Fort Monroe, Viola's position was transferred to Fort Eustis, Virginia where she worked from 1977 to 1984. That was where Viola and my current wife, Brenda, met and worked together. In fact, Viola and Brenda carpooled with two gentlemen from Norfolk, Jessie Harrell and Percy Long, for about six years.

Below is a picture taken during our visit to Richmond, Virginia to attend Viola's mother's retirement in 1982. She had been employed as an operating room nurse for many years and participated in numerous heart transplants at the Medical College of Virginia. Mr. Jasper, Viola's stepdad retired from the Virginia Alcoholic Beverage Control Authority in Richmond, Virginia (progressing from janitor to manager). Jackey, Viola's sister was a high school home economics teacher plus head of the career and technical education program.

Jackey Tunstall (Viola's sister), John Jasper (Viola's stepdad), Addie Jasper (Viola's mother), Viola Collins, March 30, 1982

In December 1985, Viola applied and was accepted for a position at Fort Monroe. She was assigned to the same organization and worked in the same building as me. It was ideal. We commuted together, ate lunch together, and truly enjoyed that time. Working and living at or near Fort Monroe was the best-kept secret in life. The work environment was wonderful.

Friendship

Viola and I also joined the Les Hommes Social and Civic Club and enjoyed the friendship and love of the diverse membership. In fact, that's where we met and socialized with three of the main characters portrayed in the movie Hidden Figures, Katherine Johnson, Dorothy Vaughan, and Mary Jackson.

Viola and Clifton Collins Sr. at Les Hommes Social and Civic Club, circa 1981

It has always been my contention that a true friend is precious. You don't need to see them every day or even every month, but you know and feel within your heart they are truly your friend. Well, Viola and I always felt we had three sets of true friends for more than thirty years, Robert and Dorothy Adams, George and Shirley Tyler, and Howard and Dorothea Mason.

Viola Collins, Dorothy and Robert Adams, 1993

Viola and Clifton Collins Sr. and Dorothy Adams, 1993

Earlier, I spoke of Viola and my relationship with Robert Adams and his wife Dorothy while stationed at Syracuse University. Robert and I shared the love of mathematics, and Viola and Dorothy were great friends. Above are pictures of us vacationing together in Gatlinburg, Tennessee during the summer of 1993. My current wife Brenda and I visited Robert and Dorothy in 2015. Robert was battling Alzheimer's disease and passed in 2017. Dorothy continues a close relationship with Brenda and me.

Howard and Dorothea Mason remain true friends. Howard and I share life experiences in the military. For more than thirty years, Howard and Dorothea lived one block down the street from Viola and me. Howard is now eighty-eight years old and enjoys his three-wheel motorcycle while caring for Dorothea, who is suffering from dementia.

Dorothea and Howard Mason, circa 2013

Shirley and George Tyler, circa 2008

My friend George Tyler passed August 14, 2013, at the age of eighty-seven after fighting prostate cancer. For many years, we shared the love of sports. In 2020, Brenda and I helped Shirley celebrate her ninetieth birthday. Sadly, Shirley passed in 2022.

There was no occasion when we ever hung out or went to a bar together. Our relationship was couple-centric. As with our other friends, we visited each other's homes, traveled on vacations together, and accompanied each other to visit family.

Vacations

Over the years, vacationing was always high on our agenda. With the military relocating us every two to three years, we could easily augment our personally planned vacations by incorporating enjoyment time during the move. For example, the military authorized us eight days to travel the 2,700 miles from Fort Irwin, California, to my parents' home in Eastville, Virginia. We also received per diem for each member of the family, totaling nearly five hundred dollars per day. Well, we often located several Holiday Inn Hotels en route and looked for surrounding sights and entertainment. Or we simply enjoyed the hotel pool.

Other vacation type activities included our annual attendance at Virginia State University homecoming; several bus trips to North Carolina Agricultural and Technical State University homecoming with our dear friends, George and Shirley Tyler; several trips with Howard and Dot Mason including Hilton Head, South Carolina (I will never forget the alligators on the golf course); cruises to the Bahamas, Jamaica, Alaska, and Mexico; visits to Baltimore Inner Harbor, Atlantic City, San Diego, Los Angeles, Disney World, and many other locations. Viola and I even visited New Orleans for Mardi Gras in 1995 and enjoyed that once in a lifetime experience.

On one memorable occasion, my family visited my sister Barbara and her family in Winton-Salem, North Carolina. We were on our way home to Hampton, Virginia, traveling in our beautiful van which had two large bay-style windows on the driver's side. As we passed through the city of Winston-Salem, an oncoming truck lost a tire. That tire jumped the medium railing and struck the van on the handle of the driver's door and continued to rip the van open like a sardine can on the left side.

In the blink of an eye, the glass windows were turned into tiny missiles. My daughters Sharon and Janice were sitting near the first glass window and had tiny pieces of glass all over their bodies. Praise the Lord, none got into their eyes. The van was still drivable, so we followed the ambulance that took Sharon and Janice to the hospital. After removal of the glass from their bodies, none of which was serious, we covered the hole in the van with plastic and headed home. The van was completely repaired to look new again, but after that accident, Viola didn't feel comfortable riding in it again.

Federal Civil Service

After military retirement, I was selected for a Federal Civil Service position at Fort Monroe as a GS-11 budget analyst. Without a waiver, federal regulations didn't allow me to be placed into the position until six months after my military retirement. Unfortunately, my waiver request was denied.

In the meantime, I taught mathematics and statistics classes for Saint Leo University and Thomas Nelson Community College.

Once on board at Fort Monroe, I managed various budgetary funds for the Training and Doctrine Command (TRADOC), covering basically all Army

Clifton at his desk as a Federal Civil Servant, 1982

training installations in the country. I was truly blessed with my effectiveness in funding the Base-level Commercial Equipment (BCE) program. This program funds all of the commercial equipment on an installation, i.e., bulldozers, lawnmowers, road construction equipment, dump trucks, buses, etc.

Not only was I able to spend the funds allocated to TRADOC in the annual budget, but I was able to spend the uncommitted funds other major commands throughout the world failed to spend at year end. The Army always wanted to spend every dime allocated so the budget wouldn't be cut the following year. I developed a procedure whereby I was always prepared to spend any leftover funds surrendered by other Army commands. Our TRADOC installations were able to acquire a lot of needed equipment.

Accepting a promotion to GS-12, I became a management analyst for six months, but I hated the job. The duties of that position were highly sensitive and of daily interest to the TRADOC Chief of Staff and Commanding

General (CG). Various management studies were conducted and briefed. Often the CG returned from a visit of an installation and directed a study be conducted on a certain subject. After much hard work for weeks and long hours, we briefed the results, and the matter was dropped. I perceived much of our work to be a complete waste of time and requested and received approval to move back to the Budget Analyst position, retaining the GS-12 grade.

Then, with the administrative help of Ms. Queen Moore in the Civilian Personnel Office, I managed to qualify as an Operations Research/Systems Analyst (OR/SA). One of the major requirements was to have a minimum of twenty-six college credit hours in mathematics. Once I was deemed qualified for an eighteen-month rotational assignment by the Civilian Personnel Office, I applied for and obtained a GS-12 position in the Resource Operation/ System Analysis Directorate on November 4, 1985, and got promoted to GS-13 in 1987 to the dream job of my life.

I was tasked to develop cost data for all Military Occupational Specialty (MOS) and functional training in TRADOC. I and other OR/SA personnel developed Cost Estimating Relationship (CER) equations which were used to fund TRADOC installations and schools throughout the U.S. We gathered all of the cost data from the installations, stripped out the one-time cost, determined the fixed costs, and ended up with an equation in the form of fixed plus variable cost. For example, the CER equation for the artillery training of enlisted trainees at Fort Sill might have been $23,000,000 + 1,500X. In other words, the annual training budget for Fort Sill may have been $23 million dollars plus $1,500 for every trainee.

The Army, Air Force, Marine Corps, and Navy attempted to consolidate as much duplicate training as possible. For instance, why should each service conduct separate dog-handler training when all services could consolidate the training in one location? The organization was designated as the Interservice Training Review Organization (ITRO). When we met, each service provided a cost analyst, manpower analyst, an engineer, and subject-matter experts. We met at an installation, developed a common curriculum, and determined the consolidated requirement for instructors, support personnel, classrooms, billets, and equipment to conduct the training at specific locations.

Then, over a period of months, the decision was made to consolidate or not consolidate the training location. This process was taking several months and many dollars. I developed a Lotus 1-2-3 cost analysis program that allowed similar groups of personnel to travel on Monday, meet on Tuesday and Wednesday, and provide the required information to the cost analysts by noon Thursday.

As cost analysts, we fed the information into the Lotus program, briefed the group on Friday morning, and all participants were free to return home on Friday afternoon. Consequently, we were getting the studies done in a week versus months at a Department of Defense annual savings of $32 million.

My Certificate of Commendation read:

> This cost analysis program was adopted by the Army, Navy, Air Force, and Marine Corps for conducting all cost analysis for Interservice Training Review Organization, and Chairman, Joint Chiefs of Staff-directed Military Training Structure Review studies. Without this program, the Chairman, Joint Chiefs of Staff-directed Military Training Structure Review would be difficult to complete within the established 3-year timetable. Mr. Collins' suggestion reflects great credit upon him and the Fort Monroe community.

The certificate of commendation was accompanied by a monetary award.

In 1998, I was selected as the Department of Defense Distinguished Cost Analyst of the Year by the American Society of Military Comptrollers and traveled to Kansas to accept the award.

Members of Providence Baptist Church

When we moved to the Hampton area, we attended church services at Chapel #3, Langley Air Force Base. The services held at the military chapel were very similar to the typical services held in Black Baptist churches. It was apparent the Air Force ensured the chaplains assigned to Chapel #3 were Black. We truly enjoyed the services and attended for several years. A few years after I retired from the military in 1981, we decided to find a church home in the civilian community. We attended several churches and finally settled on Providence Baptist Church, Newport News, Virginia. Reverend James Gray was the pastor and a humble minister who deeply cared for the welfare of the members.

In 1995, I begin serving as a trustee and choir member. Trustee Joseph Williams, a retired Army sergeant major, had been chairman of the Trustee Board for ten years and served for an additional ten years before convincing me to accept the chairmanship. During my ten years as chairman, one of my blessed moments was when the church paid off an eleven-year loan in less than three years. Using my God-given math skills to reflect potential savings, the congregation was inspired to render the church debt-free eight years earlier than planned.

Reverend Gray was an amazing man of God. Providence became the go-to place to get help for those in need. The church was so well known for helping the downtrodden, the Newport News Social Services Department referred persons-in-need when they could no longer assist them.

What I gleaned from this experience was that God had put us there to bless others, plus when parishioners know needy people are being helped, they tend to contribute more to the church. We helped everyone who came to the door, and our benevolent funds were never exhausted. Additionally, the budgetary income and expenditures were briefed in detail at every church meeting. The members knew exactly how their tithes and offerings were being used.

Over the years, I witnessed and appreciated the kindness of people. Three instances come to mind. First, at Providence Baptist Church, there was an annual "Hallelujah Fest" for the kids in lieu of them going from house to house on Halloween. Various businesses, such as McDonald's, 7-Eleven, Hardees, and Dollar Stores, were contacted during the spring and provided more than enough goodies for the kids when Halloween rolled around in October.

Second, a local family experienced the birth of multiple babies and made the local news. Viola and I donated one of our vehicles, and two local businesses donated all needed repairs and a complete paint job.

Third, an elderly lady on Medicaid who Viola and I attempted to assist as much as possible was in severe need of dental care. A local dentist accepted her as a patient and took care of all her dental needs at a minimal cost. We assisted her in budgeting her income, and you would not believe her happiness when she was able to purchase a beautiful church outfit with her own money.

The bottom line is people are good-hearted and willing to help others.

Chapter 17

Life After Viola's Stroke

Viola Suffers Stroke in 1995

Viola and I were both working in the same building at Fort Monroe and life was going very well. All the kids had left the nest. I decided I was going to finally buy a motorcycle. When I informed Viola of my intention, she stated, "You must be out of your mind to kill yourself on a dangerous motorcycle and leave me here alone with children and grandkids scattered all over the country."

Long story short, I ended up with what I call my four-wheel motorcycle—my 1994 Dodge Dakota pickup. I have truly enjoyed my four-wheel motorcycle for the past twenty-nine years.

My little Red 1994 Dodge Dakota Pickup, (my 4-wheel motorcycle)

One Wednesday afternoon, my sister Delores was visiting from New York, and Viola and I led her to a house in Phoebus, Virginia, where Viola had purchased several dolls from a lady in the past. Viola and I were riding in my pickup truck. When I parked and went around to Viola's side to assist her out of the truck, I noticed she stumbled. She assured me she was okay, but I commented she was walking like her older mother.

When we reached the house porch, Viola chose to sit on the porch rather than to enter the house. I felt something was wrong but didn't know what. The next morning, Viola was quieter than normal so I took her to the doctor. The doctor surmised she had a bad cold and would get better. That was on Thursday.

By Saturday morning, I concluded something more serious was wrong. I took her back to the same doctors' office where she was seen by a different doctor, Dr. Ollie T. Adcock.

It took Dr. Adcock less than ten minutes to diagnose Viola had suffered a stroke. Immediately, an ambulance was called to take Viola to Riverside Hospital in Newport News where we stayed for nine days. By the fifth day in the hospital, Viola had lost the use of her left side. Had the stroke being diagnosed earlier, perhaps the damage wouldn't have been as serious.

At the end of nine days in the hospital, Viola was transported to the Riverside Rehabilitation Institute in Newport News, where she stayed for five and a half weeks. I stayed with her for nine days in the hospital, and again stayed with her for the complete five and a half weeks in the rehabilitation center, 24/7. I requested her room to be declared private and secured an Army cot with an air mattress as my bed. I accompanied her in every aspect of her stay—dining, exercising, speech therapy, occupational therapy—and provided all of her personal needs, including bathing. I never wanted her to feel alone.

I often took Viola outside and pushed her in the wheelchair along the waterfront of the Chesapeake Bay. You don't really know what a person means to you until a tragedy occurs. Caring for her every need was a blessing to me, and I will always cherish our time together fighting the challenge.

Because I stayed with Viola, I made an agreement with the rehabilitation facility officials to pay thirty dollars per day to eat and use their facilities for my care. Every evening, I took my air mattress to the basement to inflate it for the night. Walmart was kind enough to exchange the air mattress every time it sprang a leak. As God would have it, upon Viola's discharge, the facility deemed my bill to be zero. Praise the Lord!

Fifteen years later, my son Clifton and I visited a TEWC (The Edge Worship Centre) church member at the same rehabilitation center and, to my surprise, a nurse still remembered Viola and me. When Viola suffered the stroke, fellow workers donated enough of their vacation time such that Viola remained on the payroll for more than a year. That was a testimony of how highly regarded Viola was among her fellow employees.

Viola's Care

At the time of Viola's stroke, I was teaching an evening class at Langley Air Force Base for Saint Leo College. I stopped teaching the evening classes for the entire seven subsequent years Viola lived. My kids Sharon and Michael were in the area and were a great help to me in caring for their mother. I hired ladies to care for her during the day and took over those responsibilities at night. Trudy Johnson and Rosetta Randall are the two ladies who come to mind. Rosetta moved in with us for a time.

Viola was very easy to care for because she was always upbeat and never complained. After four years, our daughter Janice decided to quit her job in Atlanta, Georgia, and moved to Hampton to take over the care of her mother. They were like two peas in a pod (smile). She had an apartment less than ten minutes away. Between Sharon, Janice, Michael, and myself, Viola received the best of care and love. Clifton lived out of the area but was always there during emergencies. Ronald and Donald were in the Air Force.

On a typical day, I arose at five a.m., showered, and shaved. Then I got Viola up and assisted with her shower. Once out of the bathroom, I dressed her, unrolled and combed her hair, put on her earrings, and got her ready for the day. By seven-thirty, the caretaker arrived, and I went to work.

At five-thirty p.m., I returned home to take over the caretaker duties. Of course, Viola always welcomed me loudly and joyfully. After dinner and near bedtime, I rolled her hair and readied her for bed. Because she was diabetic, I massaged her feet every night. I remember very vividly, one night, Viola woke me to assist her to do something, and I moaned and groaned. She was very apologetic she had awakened me. Well, I felt so guilty for hurting her feelings that I prayed to God to never moan and groan again when awaken. Praise the Lord, from that day forward, I always responded to her wishes in a very positive and caring manner. That was nothing but God because I was normally a heavy sleeper.

Although we had gone on a previous Alaskan cruise, we decided to take another one while Janice was home with us. Because we were provided a handicap-accessible cabin on the ship, it was at least fifteen feet wide by twenty feet long. The exterior wall was completely see-through. Viola could lie in bed and view the mountains and their wildlife, the ice glaciers, and other sights. We also had the luxury of sitting on the balcony for even better views. Janice took full advantage of room service. Reaping generous tips, the room service staff took excellent care of us. Except to attend shows and other interesting activities on the ship, we didn't have to leave our cabin.

I took Viola with me most of the time when I was required to go on trips for my job. I informed the host(s) of the meetings that my availability to attend depended on their ability to accommodate my handicapped wife. For instance, I needed a handicap parking space, a handicap-accessible meeting area, and a high back reclining chair for her to rest while I participated in the meeting activities. Often they stated my requirements couldn't be met until I made it clear that I couldn't leave her home, consequently, I would not be in attendance. Well, it always worked out.

I never wanted to leave her home when it was possible to take her with me on official trips. Sometimes the trip was canceled at the last minute, and I had to eat the cost of Viola's airline ticket, but it was worth every dime. I always wanted her to know that I never wanted to be apart from her. Her happiness was most important.

Traveling on some airplanes was a challenge, primarily because the bathrooms were small. I had to literally block the bathroom door while Viola used the facility because there was not enough internal space for both of us. I had to hold onto her because no one wanted to sit on the dirty commode. Often, if there were empty seats in first class, the stewardess allowed us to occupy those seats.

Another wonderful custom was our unplanned activities. Often, when I arrived home on Friday evening, I asked Viola, "Where are we going this weekend?"

She responded, "Wherever."

I flipped a coin. "Heads north, tails south." Whatever the result was, we threw a suitcase, her wheelchair, and other items in the back of my little red pickup and headed out first thing Saturday morning.

The agreement was whenever she felt tired, we immediately stopped, got a hotel room, and relaxed. The distance and location didn't matter. One of the major trips we enjoyed this way took us two weeks. We traveled Highway 85 south for a week and ended up at Fort Jackson, South Carolina. Along the way, we stopped and spent time at places of interest. Then, we made the return trip on Highway 95 north. We took our time getting up in the morning, had breakfast, and then headed out, always emphasizing that distance and time traveled didn't matter. It took us a solid week to reach home, and we enjoyed every minute of it.

During the seven years of Viola's life after the stroke, I did everything I could to make her happy. For instance, she had her hair styled every week, a manicure every two weeks, and a pedicure every four weeks

Mr. Pride was a member of Providence Baptist Church and owned a ladies' store on Mercury Boulevard in Hampton, Virginia. He traveled to New York periodically and returned with beautiful dresses and apparel. Viola and I shopped at his store for the best outfits. When she stepped into the church, heads turned, and she glowed. If I had to make an announcement as Trustee Chairman, I gave honor to Jesus, the pastor, my Viola, and lastly, the congregation. Viola grinned from ear to ear.

Viola had a strong love for doll babies and clowns. Every time I traveled for work or on special occasions, I purchased her either a doll baby or a clown. Presently, I have a curio full of miniature clowns. Upon Viola's death in 2002, I gave all the dolls to my daughters and granddaughters.

Viola lived for seven years after suffering the stroke. In those seven years, we continued to live as close to normal as possible, traveling and enjoying life together.

Sometimes, during my career at Fort Monroe, I felt as though my qualifications were not valued as much as others. However, looking back on it now, I realize God was in control of the situation and guided my steps in the right direction. As an example, I have given a lot of thought to how thankful I am I didn't get the promotion I wanted so badly.

I was working at Fort Monroe in a GS-13 non-supervisory position. In other words, I didn't have any supervisory responsibilities. I thought it was unfair not being promoted to GS-14, which did entail supervisory responsibility. In hindsight, I'm glad I wasn't promoted. Had I received the promotion, I couldn't have taken the time to properly care for Viola after her stroke. Every day at quitting time, I could leave work and go home to care for my dear wife. I didn't have to worry about anyone's workload but my own. Non-promotion turned out to be a blessing.

Moreover, I believe God prompted my supervisor to award me accelerated monetary step-increases which provided income comparable to or perhaps more than the average GS-14 position. Rather than accepting the routine annual bonuses, I simply requested consideration of receiving an annual step-increase, the gift that keeps on giving.

After nineteen years, I decided to retire from Federal Civil Service with an effective date of December 1, 2001. Application of my accumulated sick leave allowed me to actually depart in September. My retirement celebration was held at the Holiday Inn in Hampton, Virginia, on September 11, 2001 and I was wondering why the attendance was so low. Little did I know the events of 9/11 were taking place at that time.

To better care for my wife, I sold our two-story home in Hampton and purchased a handicap-accessible townhouse in Yorktown in December 2001. Viola loved the new home. Once she was prepared for the day, she rode her motorized chair into the sunroom and marveled at the beauty of the rising sun.

Viola's Death

Three months into our new home, Viola passed away on March 3, 2002, due to diabetic complications and kidney failure. Her death was a shocker. I didn't see it coming so suddenly. I had always been a devoted father and husband, and Viola and I had a relationship unsurpassed by anyone. She will forever hold a special place in my heart. We had been married for forty-one years and raised six wonderful children.

Viola's home-going service was truly a celebration of life. There were no outbursts of emotion or despair within the family or the congregation. Attendees felt uplifted in their spirit and stated they were leaving the service encouraged.

The following tribute was read:

> Many of you think you knew "my baby," Viola. But to truly know her, you had to be around her 24 hours a day, seven days a week, for nearly 42 years. To say that she loved the Lord, me, our children, her sister, and other members of the family, friends, doctors, etc., etc., is an understatement. Her faith and belief in the Father, Son, and the Holy Spirit exuded from every pore of her fragile body. A stroke in 1995 broke her body but never broke her spirit. My wife, lover, friend, and buddy was truly "an amazing lady." I will surely miss her, but soon and very soon, she and I will continue our love affair in the presence of our Heavenly Father.

I informed our six children while they were all home for the home-going services that I didn't intend to remain alone, and I would eventually remarry. I also promised I would not run from woman to woman, but when there was someone who appeared to meet my criteria, I would date that person. Beginning even at the repast for Viola, interested ladies attempted to get my attention. All invitations for dates, dinners, and vacations were respectfully turned down.

I enjoyed a wonderful marriage all of my adult life, therefore, I didn't wish to remain single. Viola and I had discussed this matter on many occasions. As I had to let my experiences in Vietnam and the loss of my mother and father go, I had to also let Viola go and only keep the good memories. If I had dwelled on the downside of the loss of my wonderful wife of forty-one years, it would have eaten me alive. She was my life and breath for forty-two years, including our premarital dating period. Nothing or anyone could erase that.

Jacqueline Tunstall, circa 1995

Viola's only sibling, Jacqueline Tunstall, continues to be a true blessing to me and her nephews and nieces. She constantly demonstrates love and maintains an extraordinary relationship with us.

Subsequent to the loss of Viola, I managed to stay extremely busy exercising, tutoring, and attending church activities. I am and have always been a one-woman man. Sure, I could have been a player and sociable with more than one lady, but that is not me. I informed my kids I would be cordial with everyone until I decided whom I wanted to get to know better.

Following Viola's death, Ralph Kelly, one of the church members who worked at the Fort Monroe gym, encouraged me to exercise at the fitness center and, hopefully, cope better with my loss. I began going to the gym every week. My progress was remarkable. I had not participated in a formal fitness program since my retirement from the military in 1981.

At sixty-two years old, I only suffered from minor high blood pressure

(140/80) and high cholesterol (lowered from 240 to 180). My workout schedule consisted of thirty to thirty-five minutes on the treadmill daily and resistance training on twelve Cybex machines on Monday, Wednesday, and Friday. I dabbled with free weights sometimes.

After four months, the fitness center posted my progress on their bulletin board. There was a dramatic increase in cardio endurance, stamina, and heart and other muscle strength. At the same speed and incline on the treadmill, my heart rate had decreased from 127+ beats per minute to less than 100. Muscle strength had doubled or better on all of the resistance machines—rowing weight from 60 to 140 pounds, Cybex pull-down from 80 to 210 pounds, and leg press from 140 to 260 pounds.

Chapter 18

Marriage to Brenda Edmonds-Brown

For several weeks after Viola's death, I received invitations from various ladies to join them for dinners, social events, vacations, or simply plain conversation. I didn't accept any. My kids and grandkids showered me with love and company. I felt at peace that I had done my best for Viola and myself, not only during her challenges after the stroke but throughout our life together.

About six weeks later in April, I received a call from a lady Viola and I had known for several years; she and Viola had worked together at Fort Eustis and carpooled for a time. That lady was Brenda Edmonds-Brown. Clifton Jr. had called to tell her of Viola's death. When Brenda called me, she inquired about how I was doing, knowing Viola and I were extremely close. We also shared stories of the years we had known her.

A couple of weeks later, I saw Brenda at Fort Monroe and tooted my horn to get her attention. She ignored the toot, and later I called to ask why she ignored me. She hadn't recognized my car. I went on to ask her about her longtime courtship with a mutual friend. After that discussion, I concluded their relationship was not very strong. I also learned Brenda had been married and divorced over twenty-five years earlier to William Brown Sr.

On May 8, 2002, I asked Brenda to have lunch with me, and she countered by suggesting dinner. On Friday, May 10, 2002, we had our first date at a quaint restaurant, Indian Fields Tavern, in Charles City, Virginia. I was as nervous as a sixteen-year-old en route to the prom, and it was quite obvious. We still laugh about that first date.

Brenda was scheduled to accompany her boyfriend on a cruise in two weeks, May 25, 2002. By May 20, I realized she was special, and she felt the same way about me. She wasn't going on that cruise if I could help it. I presented Brenda with a card that stated, "Follow Your Heart," and signed it, "Love, Cliff."

That same evening, Brenda called to inform me she wasn't going on the cruise. The rest is history.

On June 22, 2002, the family had a planned trip to Branson, Missouri. I decided to take Brenda on the trip. The week in Missouri was wonderful—lots of volleyball, horseshoe throwing, and my favorite activity, the go-cart races. Brenda and I even had the opportunity to attend a Charley Pride show. Do an internet search on him if you aren't familiar with him; he's an interesting man.

Prior to my first date with Brenda, I had prayed for a new wife who possessed six qualities: 1) a Christian, 2) reasonably healthy, 3) pleasant to look at, 4) no bad grownup children, 5) financially secure and not looking for a sugar daddy, and lastly, 6) between forty-five and fifty-five years old.

There were several reasons for that prayer. First, I had been a Christian since I was thirteen years old. I didn't want to create a conflict of beliefs with my future wife.

Next, Viola and I shared an amazing life journey and even illness could not diminish our love for each other. When praying for a reasonably healthy wife, my mind reflected on the wonderful times we experienced prior to her stroke. However, I knew that I would gladly repeat the same type of loving care with my future wife that I spent with Viola during her medical challenges over the years, if the need arose.

Thirdly, I didn't request beauty, only pleasant looks (received beauty) (smile). Next, I didn't wish for troublesome grown children to make our life difficult. Next, I didn't want a wife who was simply marrying me for financial support. And, lastly, I was sixty-two years old in reasonably good health and felt a lady between forty-five and fifty-five would be a great fit for me.

Well, I hadn't given my prayer much thought when, on October 7, 2002, I asked Brenda if she would marry me. She said yes. I told her our wedding would probably take place in about eight months, around June 2003. There were several reasons I chose this date. Viola had died in March so I deemed it to be too soon. I didn't want to get married in December because Viola and I had gotten married that month, and April wouldn't work because that was

Viola's birth month. So, I figured June 2003 was a good time. Brenda stated she would wait as long as necessary.

Well, two weeks later, on Wednesday, October 23, 2002, I was alone in my condo preparing for Bible study and the Holy Spirit came over me and asked, "What are you waiting for? You did all you could for your wife. What are you waiting for?"

I responded in my spirit that Viola had passed only six months ago, and people would think badly of me getting married so soon.

The Holy Spirit asked, "Who are you worried about, Me or people?"

I responded I could handle people but could not handle Him.

"Then, what are you waiting for? I gave you what you asked for."

I then considered the six qualities I had prayed my future wife would possess. 1) Christian—Brenda had a strong belief in God, 2) Healthy—she took only an aspirin periodically, 3) Pleasant to look at—she is very attractive, 4) No bad children—she had a sweet married daughter and loving son, 5) Financially secure—the mortgage was her only bill, and lastly, 6) Between forty-five and fifty-five years old—she was exactly fifty years old when we went on our first date. Brenda met every one of the six prayer requests. I then read 1 Corinthians, chapter seven, where Paul talks about marriage.

Subsequently, I thanked God and proceeded to Brenda's home where I asked her if she would agree to marry me sooner, in three weeks on November 16.

Brenda, obviously at a loss for words, blurted out, "I don't even have a dress."

I responded if she took care of getting the dress, I would take care of the rest. By the end of the following day, I had arranged for the church, preacher, caterer, and photographer.

When Brenda and I married, she joined me as a member of Providence Baptist Church, Newport News, Virginia. I was a trustee and later became the chairman for ten years. After stepping down as chairman, we continued worshipping there.

In the meantime, Clifton Jr. had become a pastor in Williamsburg, Virginia. Later, he birthed The Edge Worship Centre (TEWC) in West Point, Virginia. In 2015, Brenda and I decided to join TEWC and make the forty-five-minute trip on Interstate 64, often several times a week. It was a great decision. It's a unique pleasure to think and speak well of your pastor when the pastor happens to be your son. The congregation overall is a loving family.

Reverend Clifton Collins Jr. is a very spiritual, kind, loving, compassionate, and devoted pastor who serves his congregation well. It's an awesome pleasure to sit under the pastorship of your son who you feel within your heart and soul that he was truly called to preach the Word. Reverend Collins has clearly provided a vision for the church and the evidence of fulfillment is obvious as time passes. We truly enjoy the worship and fellowship.

Over the years, it has become quite obvious that Brenda is a leader among her siblings and other family members. She has been the anchor for the family during the sickness and loss of three brothers and continues to assist and advise her remaining siblings.

Before marriage, Brenda was a very independent self-sufficient lady with one married daughter, Kimberly, and a son, William. Kimberly is a determined individual destined to achieve her goals in life. When I married her mother, she quickly accepted me as a father figure and asked if she could refer to me as "Papa Cliff." She trusted us—and me in particular—to keep their two young boys while she was serving on active duty in Kuwait. In the meantime, her husband, Eric took care of two older children while stationed at Fort Jackson, South Carolina.

William is a wonderfully warm, mentally challenged, young man who is a pleasure to be around. When I married his mother, he and I hit it off immediately. He loves "Papa Cliff" and I love him. He fell in love with my spaghetti, so our picture on a later page reflects the beginning of our spaghetti preparation. William resides at a group-home and visits us overnight at least once a month. Of course, the coronavirus pandemic has put a hold on his visits and that's tough on him. He seriously looks forward to the Christmas holidays and probably didn't understand why he couldn't visit home during the pandemic.

With God and Love, the Collins Family Came Together

When we got married, I was sixty-three and Brenda was fifty-one years old. After only four years, Brenda retired from the federal government with thirty-five years of service. So, since 2006, we have enjoyed the blessing of living as a retired couple.

She has been and continues to be a wonderful, caring, and loving wife. Her loyalty to me and our relationship has never been a matter of concern. There is absolutely nothing I wish to change. I am indeed a happy husband and do my utmost to keep her happy.

There are no secrets between us. Our family members realize anything said to one will be shared with the other spouse. Communicate, communicate, and communicate. In addition, we both actively insist everyone in the family shows the utmost respect towards our spouse. Above all, we keep God first and do everything in love. We try to out-love each other, and there's always enough love to spread around.

Brenda Edmonds-Brown and Clifton Collins Sr,
married November 16, 2002

When two families are successfully blended, the positive qualities gained by both families far outweigh any negative. I have six adult children, twelve grandchildren, and five great-grandchildren while Brenda has two adult children, six grandchildren, and three great-grandchildren, not to mention numerous siblings and relatives. The dynamics of blended families involve not only the married couple but everyone within their realm of love.

Most importantly, the children became "our children," and every decision must be a mutual agreement. The greatest barrier is the acceptance of the newlyweds by the families. The most important participants are the married couple themselves who have the responsibility of ensuring the blending adds to the happiness and love of both families. There must be no negative actions toward or comments about each other's family. Always be slow to speak and think carefully before saying anything that could cause misunderstandings.

My advice to any married couple is to love each other until one of you says, "Please, no more!"

That day has not come in my sixty-one years of marriage. There's one thing I know for sure: the sun came up this morning, therefore, I know God is sitting high and looking low. 1 Corinthians 13:4-7 states, "Love is patient, love is kind, it does not envy, it does not boast, it is not proud. It does not dishonor others, it is not self-seeking, it is not easily angered, it keeps no record of wrongs. Love does not delight in evil but rejoices with the truth. It always protects, always trusts, always hopes, always perseveres."

Brenda and I continue to travel and enjoy our life together. We have been to various countries to include United Arab Emirates, Holland, England, Greece, Switzerland, Belgium, Germany, France, Italy, Panama, Mexico, Montenegro, Austria, Aruba, Jamaica, Puerto Rico, Virgin Islands, Canada, and just about all fifty states. Some of our most memorable trips include Hawaii, California, Florida, the Midwest National Parks, and the New England States.

Of course, due to the coronavirus pandemic, all of our planned trips were canceled for nearly two years.

Brenda and Clifton Collins Sr, circa 2015

Chapter 19

Disposition of Parents' Home

After our father moved out of the homestead in 1991, my siblings and I rented out the house for about eight years, but often the rent was not paid, and the house was a wreck when we finally evicted the tenant.

The immediate consensus was to demolish the house and put a modular home on the land. I didn't feel good about that idea because I felt a strong connection to my memories of being raised in that house. My sister Delores agreed, and we bought our siblings' share of the property. We had the house renovated in 2007. Mr. Maurice Weeks and his employees did a magnificent job. After completion of the renovations, Delores and I purchased appliances and several pieces of furniture.

Then my wife, Brenda, and I took a U-Haul truck to Delaware to pick up appliances and furniture donated by my deceased Aunt Minerva's (Uncle Earl's wife) family. We then traveled to Maryland to pick up furniture and household items from the home of Delores's late husband, Jack Thornton, and our niece Chrissy. My brother Melvin joined us from Virginia Beach, Virginia, with a trailer to transport the items. Fully furnished and ready for occupancy, we provided a key to the house to our siblings and several cousins, and we all enjoyed our "vacation" home for thirteen years.

Front view of Homestead before Renovation

Front view of Homestead after Renovation

Rear view of Homestead before Renovation

Rear view of Homestead after Renovation

During those years, my siblings and I sponsored a large cookout for family and friends every Memorial Day weekend. There was always plenty of food, music, games, and prizes for more than a hundred folks. We invited our friends and those of our parents, our former elementary and high school teachers, and anyone who wanted to come. The cookout became an annual highlight event anticipated by many on the Eastern Shore.

We sold the homestead in December 2019. Delores and I didn't visit the homestead as often at that time because most of our relatives and family friends on the Eastern Shore had passed away. The gentleman who completed the renovation and who we had been depending on for maintenance passed in 2016.

The main impetus to sell was the fact that an eighty-four-acre solar farm was built across the road from our homestead. Delores and I decided selling the home was our best option. The furniture and household items were donated to our home church, Bethel A.M.E. in Eastville, Virginia. Church members did all the work to clear the items from the house.

Chapter 20

Love of Teaching

After obtaining my master's degree from the University of Southern California in 1978 and while assigned to Fort Monroe, teaching mathematics classes for Saint Leo University became my passion. As an adjunct professor, I taught a class during the lunch hour at the Fort Monroe Education Center and/or at night either at Fort Monroe, Langley Air Force Base, or Fort Eustis. I simply love to teach mathematics. I often declare I'd rather teach mathematics than bowl or play golf. Over the years, I have not only taught for Saint Leo College, but also Thomas Nelson Community College, and most recently, Strayer University for eighteen years until the COVID pandemic. Now, at the ripe age of 83, I tutor mathematics for Bryant & Stratton College.

Clifton Collins Sr. in a Strayer University Classroom

Helping someone get over their fear of mathematics is a true joy. I take great pride in making mathematics fun for my students and changing their hate for mathematics into love for mathematics. To eliminate students' excuses such as unavailability of the instructor, every student receives my email address and telephone number. On several occasions, while traveling on the highway, I actually stopped at rest stop areas to conduct discussions with my students. Having a student feel that I am always available is my goal. This demonstration of concern has paid major dividends. For example, every student in my last two classes achieved a final grade of "A."

One of my hobbies today is collecting old math books (copyright pre-1900). The oldest book I possess was copyrighted in 1863. Nearly 160 years later, I often display that book to my mathematics and statistics students to demonstrate how terms may be different, but mathematics has not changed. My goal is to remove the mystery of mathematics and encourage my students to achieve understanding rather than memorization of concepts and to earn an "A" grade.

A quote from this student evaluation epitomizes my intention:

> Prof. Collins is indisputably the best teacher I have EVER had! I mean that truthfully and sincerely! He was able to explain the material SEVERAL different ways, which was a HUGE help for a good majority of the class. He, on his own time and with his own money prior to the quarter beginning, created note packets for the entire class. This was, as he stated, to ensure that the class was able to follow along with him rather than spending time taking notes, risking falling behind and missing something. This was an enormous help! It was unimaginably beneficial! Additionally, he gave his email, home phone number, and cell number to the class to be able to call for questions. He gave times that he was available, (which was fairly early in the morning to 10 p.m.)! The only exception was a two-hour time period on Sunday as he would be in church. He is an exceptional teacher and sets the example that other professors and teachers alike should strive to emulate. He sets the bar beyond the highest level and gets all students to the point where they may clear it with ease.

Chapter 21

Medical Challenges

It's important to know your family medical history. For that reason, I will discuss this subject in some detail.

Prostate Cancer

My family history suggested prostate cancer was prevalent. In November 2000, I learned I had prostate cancer because my Prostate-Specific Antigen (PSA) value had jumped from 2.2 to 3.8 from the year before. So, since it had increased, my doctor recommended a deeper look, meaning a biopsy. He gave me the option of periodically rechecking my PSA and noting the trend or immediately doing a biopsy of my prostate. Being mindful of my family history, I decided to undergo a biopsy.

During my follow-up visit, all the evidence suggested that my tumor was probably localized to the prostate and had not spread at that stage of the game, which meant it was a potentially curable cancer. And cure could be achieved through one of two major ways. One was to remove the prostate surgically; the second way was to treat it with radiation.

The good thing about surgical removal for someone as young as me, sixty-one years old, was it removes all of the prostatic tissue, the cancerous and non-cancerous, to avoid the potential to develop into cancer ten years down the road.

The downside to surgery is probable incontinence and sexual challenges. The other option was radiation from a source outside of the body . . . beaming radiation towards my prostate or implantation of radioactive seeds. The downside to radiation therapy, according to my doctor, was two-fold.

First, you don't know exactly where you stand with the cancer. With surgery, you can look at the cancer in detail, where it is, where it's going, and how extensive it is. With radiation, you have to make some suppositions that the cancer is at a certain stage.

The other downside is there's increasing evidence that, while radiation is very effective at times, after about thirteen to fifteen years, there is a rise in the PSA and the disease reoccurs. Not in everyone, but radiation is not 100 percent successful.

Radiation can change the tumor to a less aggressive cancer. Instead of growing in six to eight years, it may take up to sixteen to eighteen years, but you are still dealing with cancer. If I were older, like seventy, and going to live to eight-five, radiation may work for me, but at sixty-one and wanting to live to eight-five, surgery was probably the best option. So, if I were his brother or his dad, the doctor would tell me to have the surgery and be around for the next twenty years or so.

I told him if there was a high probability of being cancer-free, I could live with the incontinence and sexual challenges. He told me to go home, discuss it with my wife, and let him know my decision. Needless to say, I informed him I didn't need more time. Surgery was my choice.

I am a firm believer, if given the options of prostate removal versus radiation, removal is the better choice. Now, perhaps, if there is evidence the cancer is not confined to the prostate gland, then radiation might be the better option. That's why it is soooo important to get checked early and hopefully detect cancer early if present.

Being eighty-three years old and twenty-two years post-surgery, I am still doing well, praise the Lord. I have not regretted the decision to undergo surgery. Additionally, the Veteran Administration (VA) has declared prostate cancer as a presumptive condition due to exposure to Agent Orange during the Vietnam War. Therefore, on April 29, 2002, the VA granted me a 60 percent disability rating, which means I was awarded priority-one status for health care at VA facilities.

Heart Problem

Brenda and I were vacationing in Las Vegas with my sister Delores in 2005. As we walked from casino to casino, we noticed I couldn't keep up. I was asking them to allow me to rest for a few minutes before walking on. Well, Sunday night, when Brenda and I deplaned at the Norfolk airport and walked up the ramp to the waiting area, I had to stop and sit for a few minutes before proceeding.

Needless to say, I rushed to the doctor's office the next day. The doctor commented I didn't normally complain, therefore, he was going to send me for tests. While undergoing the stress test, the resident doctor stated there was a blockage in the back part of my heart.

Subsequently, I was referred to a cardiologist who practiced at Sentara Hampton General Hospital and speedily made an appointment. During my check-in with the nurse, I was informed the cardiologist was not available, but I would be seen by another medical doctor on his staff. I was also informed the normal option was to have the cardiologist take a look intravenously and if I needed a stent, be sent to Sentara Norfolk General Hospital to have it installed. Well, thanks to God, after talking to the staff doctor, she said, "Why don't you have the cardiologist at Sentara Norfolk General Hospital conduct the intravenous procedure, and if you need a stent, they can take care of it at the same time?"

Well, that's what happened. On March 14, 2005, at Sentara Norfolk General Hospital, I was lying on the surgical table looking at my heart pulsating on the same screen as the cardiologists, and when they saw the blockage, one of the doctors stated, "There it is!"

They inserted the stent and bang, I immediately saw the drastic increase in blood flow.

Thank God, I have had no further heart concerns until several years later when I was diagnosed with an Atrial Fibrillation condition and an ischemic heart disease. The Veteran Administration has deemed the disease to be a result of my exposure to Agent Orange in Vietnam. Consequently, I was granted a 100 percent disability rating in February 2014.

Back Problem

Beginning in 2007, I began to suffer severe pain down the back of my left leg. Twice, the doctor gave me injections of cortisone in my spine which relieved the pain for several months, but it always returned. When I decided additional shots were not a great idea, I visited several surgeons to discuss back surgery. I will never forget one surgeon who recommended the replacement of a vertebrae disk with metal and screws.

Well, finally, I met with a young surgeon who took the time to show me the x-rays and explained that he was 95 percent sure he could fix the problem by simply snipping a small piece off of two vertebras to allow more room for the nerve. I took that route and have suffered only two episodes of severe pain since, and we were on vacation both times. Before I elaborate on those two episodes, I must tell you about my stay in the hospital.

Surgery on my back was deemed a great success, however, when the operating room staff inserted the caterer, they punctured a hole through my ureter. So, when I went to the bathroom for the first time, I urinated what looked like pure blood. The amount of blood in my urine appeared to have gotten less in three to four days, and the hospital attempted to discharge me. Brenda and I decided there was still too much blood in my urine and eventually had to contact Medicare to get authorization to remain a couple of days longer.

On the first day home, Brenda had given me a dose of Epsom salts for constipation. When I got the urge to go, I sat on the commode and couldn't urinate. Eventually, I directed Brenda to call 911. Instead, she decided to lay hands on me and pray. Because I had taken a laxative, I experienced an unusually strong urge to urinate, and a blood clot popped out, followed by a normal urine flow. The clot appeared to be star-shaped and an inch in diameter. I didn't suffer any further problems with blood in my urine, thanks to God for answering Brenda's prayer.

Back-related Pain Episodes

Now, to my two back-related pain episodes. One time I had trimmed my hedges on Wednesday and was scheduled to depart on a week-long cruise on Saturday. Well, that twisting motion at the waist obviously agitated my back. Once on the cruise ship on Saturday, I went to the dining area for dinner. When I returned to my cabin, I was in such pain, I could barely make it to the bathroom when nature called. Even after the onboard doctor provided pain medication, I was still completely bedridden for the entire week-long cruise.

Every day of the cruise, Brenda went to the dining hall and brought my food to the cabin. I could barely tolerate getting up to visit the bathroom.

The other painful episode occurred as the result of bending over and twisting while washing my truck. Two days later, we were on vacation in San Antonio, Texas, visiting our son Ronald. Brenda and I had secured a wonderful hotel room in the Hilton Hotel on the San Antonio River Walk. All we had to do was go down the escalator onto the River Walk. Needless to say, I was bedridden the entire week and never ventured onto the River Walk.

Those two episodes made me a believer, and I have been extremely careful of activities involving movements twisting my back.

Chapter 22

Life Lessons

Another thing I enjoy doing is sharing my life lessons. Of course, often I am the recipient of life lessons, so I'm not claiming to be a know-it-all. After living eighty-three years and being married for more than sixty-one years, I have some strong feelings about life and marriage.

Too often, we fail to teach and share crucial lessons with our family and friends, most importantly, our children. I'm a proud father who feels that each son and daughter has special unique qualities and values. They are all special, and I'm truly happy and thankful to be Dad, Daddy, or Papa Cliff. I love each child wholeheartedly.

The following comments are based on my successes, failures, and lessons thus far on my journey. Believe me, I am a long way from being perfect and will be forever regretful for some of my decisions in life, however, hindsight is always 20/20. Prayerfully, this book will be enlightening and helpful to every reader.

God in Your Marriage

The Bible talks about the man being the leader of the family. I'm not perfect, but I have attempted to always consult the Lord in prayer before any major decision is made to ensure I make the best decision at that time. Of course, again, hindsight is always 20/20. I just made the best decision at that moment in time. I have learned over the years that my wife loves for me to accept the leadership role. In my sixty-one years of marriage, I have not had to overrule my wife's preferences but a few times (smile). Once I consult the Lord and feel at peace with my decision, I discuss the matter with my wife who prayerfully provides her input. Even if she sways my final decision, it's my decision.

Men are often accused of not listening. It's not that we don't listen; we simply don't pay attention. I suggest the more we give our wives and children our undivided attention, the more they will pick and choose their times to interrupt our activities. The best communication between a husband and wife is prayer. I pray daily, but I must admit that I don't read the Bible as much as I should. We must make it our business to talk about God to our family every day. It's never too late to tell our children about our Lord and Savior.

Marriage to me is a lifetime contract. I'm determined to make it work. Divorce is not an option for me. Sure, there are rough times, but there are always going to be disagreements when there are two people involved. No two people are exactly the same in likes and dislikes. There must be a compromise.

When was the last time you told your spouse you loved him or her?

When was the last time you told each child you loved him or her?

When was the last time you told your parent(s) you love them?

Genesis 2:18 indicates marriage is God's idea. "The Lord God said, it is not good for the man to be alone. I will make a helper suitable for him."

I've learned a lot about what works and what absolutely does not work. First of all, when I married Viola and later Brenda, I made a vow that I would be faithful. That meant a lot and couldn't be taken lightly. In my first marriage, I was only twenty-one years old, and Viola nor I had any idea how to make our marriage work. The key was to communicate, communicate, communicate.

We continually held each other and expressed our love for each other, resulting in a wonderful closeness. Of course, society was our worst enemy in keeping our marriage together. There were lots of outsiders and societal activities working against us, such as unfaithful friends, parties, alcohol intake, etc.

Knowing that unfaithfulness breaks the bond of trust, I have always attempted to convey to my wife that I'm completely loyal to her in thought and deed. Adultery doesn't occur overnight. It's something that happens gradually. There are some people and/or situations we know we should stay away from or we are headed for trouble.

We all have a choice, but just be mindful and diligent about "guarding your ear-gate and eye-gate." Just as no two things can occupy the same space, whatever we constantly listen to and view can become our reality. 1 John 2:16 states, "For everything in the world—the lust of the flesh, the lust of the eyes, and the pride of life—comes not from the Father but from the world."

Please don't view my personal stories as boasting, but I praise God every day for what He has done in my life. I never participated in a "boys' night out" because being married at the young age of twenty-one, I knew my hormones were raging. Such an atmosphere may have led to my destructive behavior. That's what I consider as "living on the edge." Continuously living on the edge, you will eventually fall off. When guys teased me about being henpecked because I didn't hang with them, I simply stated I was going home to get some more of that good pecking.

God always provides a way to escape the wiles of the devil. For example, when I went on business trips, I took my wife when possible. In Vietnam, I wrote letters to her just about every day. That helped me maintain my focus. Plus, I can only imagine the strain on her, knowing her husband and father of six kids was in harm's way daily.

Later, when Viola suffered the stroke, I not only remained faithful, but I did whatever it took to make her feel loved and happy. That was my way of being faithful and showing appreciation to the woman who had birthed our six children and who had put up with my shortcomings for years. A friend said the other day, "A happy wife means a happy life."

With the help of God and the Holy Spirit, I can keep my vows and rejoice every day for being a Godly man.

When Viola died, I could have decided to date every available lady, but I'm very glad I didn't. I cannot even imagine the effect that activity could have had on my marriage to Brenda. Being able to declare to Brenda there was no one else after my late wife Viola was reassuring to her, and I feel good about that fact.

Often it's difficult to tell your wife she has committed an act that you don't like or failed to do something, for fear that it will hurt her feelings or make her angry. Well, I think women value honesty above everything I will mention. It's easy to struggle with honesty. There's always the fear, but I must be honest about my emotions. If there's anything I am not pleased with in my marriage, I tell my wife. If I fail to do so, I hinder the full enjoyment of our relationship by not being upfront with something that's bothering me. Chances are, the matter is remedied quite easily. Of course, the reverse is true also.

Over the years, I continually built up and edified my wife and children. I did my best to train, teach, instruct, and discipline my children, not brutalize them. I may not have known everything, but I knew more than my children did. I did my best to encourage my children, set a Godly example, and not provoke them.

There are two things I tried to give my family, time and love. Playing golf, watching a football game, or being with the guys was not more important than my wife or kids. That's the main reason I never looked for a second job while my kids were young. Time is often more important than money. When I began teaching a math class for Saint Leo in 1978, the class was conducted on Fort Monroe during the lunch hour.

It's important to laugh with each other but not at each other. I have witnessed husbands making fun of their wives in a demeaning way. While the husband was enjoying himself, the wife appeared to be laughing to keep from crying. I'm sure every time that took place, the wife lost a little more respect for her husband. The same holds true for friendship. I refrain from using my wife or friends as victims of my humor.

I have found my wife wants more than sex; she wants love, romance, and respect. Simply holding my wife may be more meaningful to her than pure sex. Of course, we are different, and I recognize that difference.

I never make negative comments about my wife or kids to others, including family members. If I ever told someone something negative about my wife or child, it would take years to erase that image. I have always tried to say only positive things about and to my loved ones. The tongue can cut deeper than a knife. Once the disrespectful words are out of my mouth, I cannot take them back.

I hold my wife's hand when we're together. I open the car door for her. To really put the icing on the cake, not only do I open her door, but I also hook her seatbelt and kiss her prior to closing her door. Viola, and now Brenda, loves it.

While raising six kids, there was no such thing as wife duties and husband duties. It was always "our" duties. I did just as many dishes, diapers, and meals as Viola, and even today, I continue to cook, wash dishes, and do other household tasks. As I stated earlier, I will pour love on my wife until she says "enough is enough." I have never been asked to stop.

Lastly, in Romans 1:28-32, Paul said that a man without God is subject to do just about anything contrary to God's Word. They even invent ways of doing evil. A godly man is a reflection of his Savior. He must have the mind of God. He must have the heart of God. We are all flawed individuals chosen by a flawless God to do His will. God has given us free will. I have found that the best days of my life have been when I did my best to live according to God's Word.

Relationship

Life is a one-way journey - There is no way to return to yesterday to make changes. You may make some mistakes, but you make the best decision at that specific time. Rest assured; hindsight is always 20/20. Don't beat yourself up for making the wrong decision, for it was the best decision at that time. Therefore, you must do the best you can each and every day.

Value of time – While working one or perhaps two jobs, attending school, or participating in other activities that consume time, you must consider the impact on your family, your health, and your happiness. Time with your loved ones is the most important. You must do your very best to maintain a balance. You must not allow anything to hinder you from spending valuable time with your loved ones.

Family – No matter how many friends you may have, there is a higher probability your family will be there when the chips are down. Count on your parents, but don't abuse the love of the family by assuming they owe you something. Everyone has the responsibility of earning their own way in life.

Be respectful of people – I often state that most of life's dynamics are similar to the dynamics of a boomerang. You receive what you put out. Treat every man as your father or brother, every woman as your mother or sister, and child as your child. You will likely receive the same level of excellent treatment.

Show Love – Don't assume your loved ones know you love them. Take every opportunity to tell your spouse, parents, children, grandchildren, siblings, cousins, friends, etc. that you love them. Always look for something positive to encourage and uplift them. For instance, over the years I have maintained Cliff's Love Bank where I continuously make deposits. Typical deposits include a gift of flowers for no particular occasion, a sincerely stated "I love you" when in a loved one's presence, a phone call, a written letter or card, a kind word, etc., etc. Make deposits to your Love Bank account daily and witness the positive impact you will have on recipients' lives.

No bad-mouthing our loved ones – We must never talk bad about our loved ones to others. No matter what happens in the future, those negative comments will come back to bite us. For example, if we speak badly about our child, spouse, or friend, no matter how much they improve in the future, our friend with whom we shared the bad comments will only remember the bad. Our loved ones will never gain the respect they deserve. Don't make comments to your friends, such as, "My husband (or wife) doesn't do so-and-so for me." Build your loved ones up directly and to others, not down. One of my favorite responses to guys teasing me about being henpecked by not hanging out with them is, "I am going home to get some more of that good pecking" (it was worth repeating).

Don't allow technology to raise your kids – Control your kids' use of technology and communicate with them. In my younger days, family communication took place around the dinner table. Today, families tend not to eat together. Even if they are dining out, everyone is concentrating on their phone or iPad, especially the kids. The time available to raise kids is very short, only about seventeen years, and you only get one shot at it. When my grandkids enter my home, their technology items are confiscated until we have had a "bring me up to date" conversation.

Live to minimize regrets – In other words, if you feel you will regret not doing something, then do it. Examples include attending special occasions such as graduations, weddings, military retirement, etc. Other examples may be visiting an old friend or telling someone you love them or they hurt your feelings.

Honesty and integrity – These attributes are very important if you wish to have a good life. You feel rejuvenated when you display honesty and integrity. It's a great feeling. My wife, Brenda, demonstrated integrity and honesty just yesterday. She shopped for several items to include a set of bed sheets. Once in the car, she kept wondering why her bill was quite lower than expected. Soon she discovered she had not been charged for the sheets. We immediately returned to the store and paid for the sheets. In doing so, she has nothing to fear or hide because she did the right thing. There is no guilt. Do the right thing and live with no regret. Did you keep the excess dollar the cashier gave you by mistake? You cannot perpetuate a lie. You will eventually get tripped up and lose whatever trust others may have had in you. You will find that you may feel bad when you fess up, but the relationship will heal quite rapidly. The other person will continue to trust you.

Finance

Join a bank or credit union – Make automatic deposits to the bank or credit union. There's a tendency to spend what you receive in your hands. However, if you don't see the money, then you won't spend it. Have an amount taken from your paycheck each pay period to be placed into an account you will not touch. Save the amount you can afford. Every little bit counts, and you'll be amazed by how fast your account will grow. If you wish to improve your credit rating, borrow a small amount, and use the loan money to make your monthly payments. Maintain funds for an emergency cushion allowing you to sleep peacefully, and don't touch it (use only for a real emergency).

Major purchases – Debt is like having an anvil around your neck. I visited a car dealer in 1984 and allowed the excitement of looking at that pretty Lincoln Town Car get me in debt well beyond what I could afford at that time. I made a promise to myself I would never make that mistake again. It feels much better to be able to spend for your needs (and some wants) without the thought of "can I afford it?" than it is to have a new car, a Rolex watch, or a big boat.

Buy your home – Chances are, if you can afford to rent, you can afford to buy. In the first ten years of a thirty-year mortgage, 90 percent of your payments go to interest; therefore, pay off your home as soon as possible. Consider biweekly payments. The monthly payment amount is the same, but it will knock years off the mortgage time.

Pay off credit cards – Don't leave a balance on your credit card. Paying the minimum on $8,400 at 18 percent will take 30.5 years to pay off at the total cost of $20,615. Beware of "quick fix" advertisers. If you need assistance, I recommend doing research to find reputable credit counseling services, which is normally free.

Use overtime pay wisely – Don't use overtime pay for living expenses. Use it wisely. Make extra payments on major bills, home mortgage, car payment balance, or put it in savings. If you get accustomed to using the overtime money for regular living expenses, it will really rock your boat when there is no more overtime.

Payday loan/title loans – Beware of "Payday Loan/Title Loan" places. A mere $500 loan may cost you five times that amount and often your vehicle. If you must use their services, beware of contracts that will not allow you to pay the loan off early and obligate you to make a set number of payments of a set amount.

Never co-sign loans – A person needing a co-signer probably has had problems making payments in the past. Don't put your credit score in jeopardy by allowing them to control the payments. One late payment by that individual will harm your credit. If you absolutely have to, be sure to control the payments.

Beware of Scams – If you are asked to send money to receive money, 99.99 percent of the time, it's a scam. Other scams include telephone calls from fake close family members in distress asking for bail money, etc. If something seems too good to be true, chances are, it is. Nothing in this world is free, and I am not referring to only money. It could be your good reputation.

Employment

Performance evaluation – Once a supervisor completes an evaluation, the chance of them making changes for the better is virtually zero. To increase your chance of receiving an excellent evaluation, always know what your future evaluation will look like. Your evaluation, good or bad, should never be a surprise to you when you receive it. Approach your evaluator to determine the exact job description. Perform the job for at least two to three weeks. Have your evaluator indicate exactly what your evaluation would be at that time. If you aren't at the very top, find out what you must do to get there. Go out and perform your job for another two to three weeks and return to your evaluator to determine if you are now meeting those goals. If you're at the top, request to be informed if you ever fall from that spot. If you're not at the top, get clarity again on what it will take to get there and perform for another two to three weeks, and so forth.

Retirement – Prepare NOW for your retirement. It is never too late to begin your preparation. Life is not promised, but we must assume we may live to a ripe old age. Although you may be making a great salary now, there will become a day when you will no longer be employed and your livelihood will depend on whatever residual income you have. We all love to help others; however, don't help others to the point where you are not helping yourself. Who will take care of you when you turn 75 or 80+ years old?

Faith

Faith – I can only speak from personal experiences. I know God exists for there is no other explanation for the existence of the universe and everything therein. God has moved in my life awesomely, and I have no doubt. He has been there every step of the way—through my young crazy days, sickness, marriage, war, sickness and death of loved ones, raising kids, etc., etc., etc. I thank God for sacrificing His son Jesus for us. Jesus is the Way. I call on God in the name of Jesus for my mere existence. I give God the credit for every moment of my life, and I lean on the Holy Spirit to guide my every step. No two things can occupy the same space. When there are negative thoughts and the Devil is at his best, call on Jesus and the Devil must flee.

Personal Care

Lastly, take care of YOU – Often we rely on the medical professionals and others to take care of us. I certainly don't know all the answers, but I will share my thoughts. First, you are your own best doctor. You know more about your health, habits, and body than any doctor who sees you once a year. You know when something is going wrong in your body. You must make every attempt not to procrastinate but take action immediately.

There were a few things I decided to do to help beat the odds and live a healthy and prosperous life. I don't smoke (stopped in my late thirties after nearly twenty-five years), limit alcohol intake to an occasional glass of wine, drink plenty of water (keep urine as clear as possible), eat lots of fruit and salads, visit the bathroom routinely, and keep a record of all lab results—cholesterol, potassium, glucose, etc. I take notice of any up or down trend in my lab results. For instance, I can tell you what my glucose level has been for the past fifteen years. So, if I notice an adverse trend, I discuss corrective actions with my doctor.

Early in 2022, I noticed my heart rate was rather slow, hovering around forty beats a minute. I informed the doctor of my concern, and eventually ended up with a pacemaker. Now, my pulse averages sixty beats per minute, and my blood pressure readings remain excellent.

The statement "use it or lose it" is very true. Several months ago, my body was getting a little flabby due to a lack of exercise and/or physical activity. I returned to my exercise regimen every other day by simply running in place for eight-plus minutes and using eight-pound weights to do 150-plus curls and other arm and chest exercises. My body has toned up rather well in a short time, and I feel energetic and happy.

Chapter 23

To Our Children

I sincerely love each of you without exception. You are simply wonderful human beings—kind, respectful, loving, compassionate, generous, and a myriad of other wonderful descriptors. You have done extremely well in life, and I am so thankful that you are my child.

I didn't dwell on your life story for fear of omitting an important aspect. Prayerfully, I hope nothing I have stated or omitted in this book will offend anyone. If so, please credit it to my head and not my heart.

Hopefully, this book will be enlightening and helpful to you and your families for many years into the future. Continue to enjoy life and keep God first in every thought and action. It has truly been a blessing to put my thoughts in writing. God bless YOU!

Love, Dad/Daddy/Papa Cliff

Clifton Collins Jr., circa 2019

Sharon Collins Curry, circa 2016

Janice Collins, circa 2015

Donald and Ronald Collins, circa 2016

William Brown and Clifton Collins Sr., circa 2014

Michael Collins, circa 2018

Kimberly Brown-Mason, circa 2019

Does God Exist?

From an unknown author

The Bible says to have an answer for why you believe to give those who ask you. The story below is a good example of an answer to one of the most common reasons people give for ignoring God and His goodness.

A man went to a barbershop to have his hair cut and his beard trimmed. As the barber began to work, they began to have a good conversation. They talked about so many things and various subjects. When they eventually touched on the subject of God, the barber said, "I don't believe that God exists."

"Why do you say that?" asked the customer.

"Well, you just have to go out in the street to realize that God doesn't exist. Tell me, if God exists, would there be so many sick people? Would there be abandoned children? If God existed, there would be neither suffering nor pain. I can't imagine a loving God who would allow all of these things."

The customer thought for a moment but didn't respond because he didn't want to start an argument. The barber finished his job and the customer left the shop. Just after he left the barbershop, he saw a man in the street with long, stringy, dirty hair and an untrimmed beard. He looked dirty and unkempt.

The customer turned back and entered the barbershop again, and he said to the barber, "You know what? Barbers do not exist."

"How can you say that?" asked the surprised barber. "I am here, and I am a barber. And I just worked on you!"

"No," the customer exclaimed. "Barbers don't exist because if they did, there would be no people with dirty long hair and untrimmed beards, like that man outside."

"Ah, but barbers DO exist! What happens is people do not come to me."

"Exactly!" affirmed the customer. "That's the point! God, too, DOES exist! What happens is people don't go to Him and do not look for Him. That's why there's so much pain and suffering in the world."

BE BLESSED and BE A BLESSING

Acknowledgment

*This project couldn't have been
completed without encouragement,
editing, proofreading, and support
of my dear wife Brenda.*

*Others who read the draft
and provided excellent feedback were*

*my siblings:
Melvin Collins, Delores Thornton
Barbara Eure, and Lafayette Collins*

*my sister-in-law:
Jacqueline Tunstall*

*and children:
Clifton Collins Jr
Sharon Curry
Janice Collins,
Ronald Collins
Donald Collins,
Michael Collins
Kimberly Brown-Mason
plus, inspiration from my son
William Brown*

*The excellent layout, format, and final editing was expertly accomplished by Dawn
Brotherton, Blue Dragon Publishing, LLC.*